AIR CAMPAIGN

THE BLITZ 1940–41

The Luftwaffe's biggest strategic bombing campaign

JULIAN HALE | ILLUSTRATED BY MADS BANGSØ

OSPREY PUBLISHING
Bloomsbury Publishing Plc
Kemp House, Chawley Park, Cumnor Hill, Oxford OX2 9PH, UK
29 Earlsfort Terrace, Dublin 2, Ireland
1385 Broadway, 5th Floor, New York, NY 10018, USA
E-mail: info@ospreypublishing.com
www.ospreypublishing.com

OSPREY is a trademark of Osprey Publishing Ltd

First published in Great Britain in 2023

A catalogue record for this book is available from the British Library.

ISBN: PB 9781472857880; eBook 9781472857873;
ePDF 9781472857866; XML 9781472857859

23 24 25 26 27   10 9 8 7 6 5 4 3 2 1

Maps by www.bounford.com
Diagrams by Adam Tooby
3D BEVs by Paul Kime
Index by Fionbar Lyons
Typeset by PDQ Digital Media Solutions, Bungay, UK
Printed and bound in India by Replika Press Private Ltd.

To find out more about our authors and books visit www.ospreypublishing.com. Here
you will find extracts, author interviews, details of forthcoming events and the option to
sign up for our newsletter.

Note:
Many German documents produced during World War II routinely refer to Britain
and the British people as 'England' and the 'English'. This mistake is reproduced when
quoted.

Times: During the winter of 1940/41, the British government decreed that the clocks
be set to British Summer Time (GMT +1). On 3 March 1941, this changed to Double
British Summer Time (GMT +2). The same format is adopted in this book.

CONTENTS

INTRODUCTION

When the perspective of time has lengthened, all stands in a different setting. There is a new proportion. There is another scale of values. History with its flickering lamp stumbles along the trail of the past, trying to reconstruct its scenes, to revive its echoes, and kindle with pale gleams the passion of former days.

Winston Churchill, House of Commons, 12 November 1940

The noise was so great on that warm, hazy morning that many later said they heard them ten minutes before they saw them. Some thought they resembled a gaggle of geese. Others compared them to a collection of 'silver specks'. Most realized they were aircraft – but presumed them to be friendly. Then the explosions began. The first bombs landed in London's East End and, when the aircraft had finished their lazy turn over Regent's Park, the remainder were released in a broad swathe across the City and docks. One 50kg bomb, after falling some two and a half miles, crashed through three floors of a school in Poplar, exploded inside a classroom and killed 18 children. The anti-aircraft guns failed to bring down any of the bombers and instead proved more dangerous to those they were trying to protect: falling shrapnel from spent shells killed two people and injured 18 more. The carnage caused by the Gothas that morning in June 1917 left 162 people dead or dying and another 432 wounded.

The raid marked the beginning of what is known as the 'First London Blitz'. In February 1917, the German High Command, stung by the airship losses of the previous autumn, authorized aeroplane attacks on Britain. Despite a modest number of aircraft, it was hoped that Operation *Türkenkreuz* ('Turk's Cross') would do enough to cause a crisis of morale in the British population. The strategic air campaign coincided with the decision to begin unrestricted U-boat warfare. Both were gambles designed to force Britain out of the war. Both ultimately failed. In this, *Türkenkreuz* shared a number of similarities with the Luftwaffe's campaign 23 years later.

This watercolour painting depicts an attack by Zeppelin airships on London in 1916. The airships, not originally intended for strategic bombing, proved expensive, accident-prone and vulnerable to improved British fighter defences. By the end of 1916, the campaign had been brought to a temporary halt. (ullstein bild/Contributor, Getty)

The Gothas had shown the potential of strategic bombing. In 1921, Italian air theorist Giulio Douhet wrote *Il dominio dell'aria* ('The Command of the Air'). His prediction that bombing could be the decisive arbiter in future conflicts gained considerable credence in some air forces. Novelists, meanwhile, free from the constraints of economic and logistical reality, were horrifying their readers with predictions of what a future war would entail. Almost invariably, these involved massive bombardments of towns and cities from the air, using not only high explosive and incendiaries, but gas as well. The military theorist, J.F.C. Fuller, thought that an air attack would reduce London's population to insanity. An RAF Air Staff estimate made in the late 1930s suggested the Luftwaffe could drop 400 tons (406.4 tonnes) of bombs a day for several weeks, or in a knock-out blow, 3,500 tons in 24 hours. Gas bombs would contribute up to 25 per cent of these respective totals. Predictions of casualties nationwide were 60,000 killed and 100,000 injured on day one, with a further 20,000 casualties for each day afterwards.

Backing up these grim predictions was the revolution in aeronautical design. Aircraft had developed from fabric-covered wooden airframes to streamlined, all-metal designs. By 1934, the American Martin B-10 monoplane boasted a top speed of 213mph, a ceiling of more than 24,000ft, a powered turret for self-defence and a bombload of 2,200lb. At the time, the RAF's premier fighter was the Hawker Fury biplane, with a top speed of 207mph.

To many, the solution to the 'shadow of the bomber' lay either with disarmament, including a ban on bombing, or with deterrence. The latter was neatly summarized in 1932 by the British Deputy Prime Minister, Stanley Baldwin:

I think it well … for the man in the street to realise there is no power on earth that can protect him from bombing, whatever people may tell him. The bomber will always get through … the only defence is in offence, which means that you have to kill more women and children more quickly than the enemy if you want to save yourselves.

This grim rationalization was to be echoed in later decades by adherents of the nuclear deterrent.

The ghastly scenarios envisaged by professional military theorists, novelists, journalists and politicians appeared to be borne out by experience. In 1932, Japanese bombers killed hundreds in Shanghai. Between 1935 and 1937, Italian bombers attacked Ethiopian forces and civilians with poisonous gas. On 26 April 1937, aircraft from the newly created German Luftwaffe, flying in support of Spanish Nationalist forces, bombed the town of Guernica, killing a reported 1,687 people (later estimates revised this to 240 killed).

The 1919 Versailles settlement had specifically banned a German air arm but the training of military aircrew was secretly arranged with the Soviet Union in the 1920s. The Nazi rearmament programme envisioned a powerful air force. In March 1935, Hitler publicly announced the existence of the Luftwaffe. The new air force would benefit not only from lavish spending programmes but also practical experience, gained in years of combat operations over Spain. Between 1935 and September 1939, boastful propaganda claims for the size and sophistication of the Luftwaffe fuelled further anxiety in Europe.

Nowhere were these concerns greater than in Britain, where memories of the airships and Gothas remained strong. The failure of disarmament talks and a desire to find an alternative to the policy of bomber deterrence led to a renewed interest in air defence. The story of the development of radar, an associated system of fighter control and the new generation of monoplane interceptors, is well known. By 1939, Britain possessed a superb daytime air defence system. The problem of night-interception, however, was still to be resolved.

Today, the Blitz of 1940–41 is, at most, a distant memory. It is regarded as a pivotal moment in modern British history, a point after which many societal questions could no longer be ignored. It is likewise true that history is written by the victors and much of the historiography of the Blitz has been written by – and for – an Anglo-American readership. Surviving British records, of which there are a great number, provide a comprehensive

The Gothas were personally led by Hauptmann Ernst Brandenburg, the commander of Kagohl 3, informally known as the 'England Geschwader'. Brandenburg secured a position in the German Ministry of Transport in the 1920s but he was considered politically unreliable by the Nazis and forced to retire in 1942. (ullstein bild/ Contributor, Getty)

bedrock for accounts which now cover almost all aspects of the campaign. Those of the Luftwaffe are far less complete. While British histories commonly view the Blitz with a degree of pride (although there are those who point to aspects which undermine the notion of the famous 'Blitz spirit'), German memoirs and scholarship have paid it only passing attention. This is due to two especial reasons. For the Luftwaffe, the Blitz (as it is understood in Britain, the bombing offensive running from September 1940 to May 1941) was merely a continuation of a campaign that had begun two months previously. There was no convenient moment at which the Battle of Britain abruptly transformed into the Blitz. This is entirely as it should be: the bombing campaign gradually emerged (in fact, re-emerged) as the Battle of Britain ground to a halt. Secondly, the Blitz stands in the shadow of two extraordinary events: the Nazi conquest of western Europe on one side and *Barbarossa*, the invasion of the Soviet Union, on the other. Indeed, Hitler never evinced much enthusiasm for the Luftwaffe's campaign and was already formulating his plans for *Barbarossa* as early as July 1940. It is therefore the aim of this history to present the 'other side' of the story in greater detail than hitherto, to examine the campaign's aims, methods and results and, finally, to show how the Blitz fits into the story, not just as an anonymous kind of bridge between two events but as the world's first, sustained, strategic bombing campaign.

CHRONOLOGY

1934

11 May The *Langstrecken-Grossbomber* (long-range heavy bomber or Uralbomber) programme is initiated.

1935

1 March The existence of the Luftwaffe is announced.

November The Uralbomber programme is downgraded to 'demonstrator' status.

1936

17 April The Luftwaffe's 'Bomber A' requirement for a strategic bomber is issued.

1938

Summer 1938 The *Flugfunkerschule und Versuchskommando* (Radio Operators' Training and Experimental Command) is formed. The unit is renamed KGr 100 Wiking in November 1939.

22 September As tensions flare during the Munich Crisis, the Luftwaffe produces a study of the feasibility of an air campaign against Britain.

1939

21 May The first trial flight of Airborne Interception radar (AI Mk I) is made in a Fairey Battle.

22 May *Studie Blau*, a report which forms the basis for Luftwaffe operations against Britain, is published.

17 July First flight of the Bristol Beaufighter prototype.

3 September War declared. Blackout imposed. The BBC shuts down regional broadcasting and the new television service to prevent their use for navigation by the Luftwaffe.

22 November Luftwaffe Intelligence chief, *Oberst* Josef Schmid, produces *Proposal for the Conduct of Air Warfare Against Britain*. The document stresses the targeting of British shipping and harbours.

29 November Führer Directive No 9 reiterates the importance of Britain's naval and mercantile assets.

December The Luftwaffe installs three *Knickebein* ('Crooked Leg') navigation beam transmitters in Germany.

20 December A KGr 100 aircraft flies to London and back to check the security of the *X-Verfahren*.

1940

Spring 1940 Several clues, gleaned from crash-landed aircraft and captured crewmen, lead Air Ministry Scientific Intelligence to deduce that the Luftwaffe is using a system of beams (in fact *Knickebein*) to locate targets over the UK.

21 June A Downing Street meeting is held to discuss the implications of *Knickebein*. That night, an Anson discovers the beams, which intersect over the Rolls-Royce factory at Derby.

27 June A decrypted Enigma message mentions 'Wotan', the *Y-Gerät* apparatus.

July 80 Wing RAF is established to coordinate radio countermeasures. The first beam-masking stations ('Meacons') begin operations.

29 July A conference is held to begin preliminary planning for Germany's invasion of the USSR.

August The first attempts to jam *Knickebein* are made, codenamed 'Aspirin'.

1 August In Führer Directive No 17, Hitler states that the Luftwaffe is to attack the aircraft industry as part of the battle for air superiority, adding: 'I reserve to myself the right to decide on terror attacks as measures of reprisal'.

13 August 21 He 111s of KGr 100 bomb Castle Bromwich using *X-Gerät*.

18/19 August The first bombs fall on London suburbs.

24 August Hitler instructs that no attacks are to be made on London without his own authorization.

24/25 August A small number of He 111s from KG 1, searching for the Thames Haven oil terminal, accidentally bomb the City.

25/26 August British bombers raid Berlin in retaliation for the attack on London. A greenhouse is damaged, injuring two people.

28–31 August The Luftwaffe attacks Liverpool on four successive nights, dropping a total of 455 tons of high explosive bombs and 1,029 containers of incendiaries.

28/29 August A second RAF raid on Berlin kills eight people.

'The Shadow of the Bomber'. The bombing of Guernica by the German Condor Legion in April 1937 attracted worldwide condemnation and inspired Picasso's famous painting. Ironically, the Luftwaffe did not believe in 'terror bombing' but the destruction of the small Spanish town dovetailed with the brutal image of the Third Reich.(Anadolu Agency, Getty)

30 August Hitler authorizes the bombing of London.

5/6 September The Luftwaffe launches its first night raid with London as the specific target.

7 September 'The Saturday': the first daylight raid on London.

16/17 September KGr 126 drop the first *Luftmines* on London.

17 September The Beaufighter Mk IF begins trials with AI Mk IV radar.

30 September The last major daylight raid on London.

29 October The *Corpo Aereo Italiano* (CAI) makes its first appearance over the UK when 15 Fiat BR 20 bombers attack Ramsgate.

6/7 November A Heinkel He 111 of KGr 100 force-lands off Bridport. The *X-Gerät* equipment aboard is recovered and examined.

14/15 November The Luftwaffe destroys the centre of Coventry.

Late November 80 Wing begins attempts to counter *X-Gerät*, using jammers codenamed 'Bromide'.

17/18, 23/24 & 30 November/1 December The 'Southampton Blitz'.

19/20 November 604 Squadron (Sqn) claim the first kill using AI radar.

The full panoply of the Third Reich, with the Luftwaffe taking centre stage, April 1939. These Heinkel He 111s were taking part in Adolf Hitler's 50th birthday celebrations. A modern and seemingly all-powerful air force was a fundamental part of the Third Reich's image. (ullstein bild/Contributor, Getty)

19–22 November & 11/12 December The 'Birmingham Blitz'.

November III/KG 26 begins intensive use of *Y-Gerät*.

2/3 December The Starfish decoy site at Stockwood, near Bristol, draws a few bombs.

12/13 & 15/16 December The 'Sheffield Blitz'.

18 December Hitler issues Führer Directive No 21: 'Case Barbarossa'.

21/22 December 23 Sqn begins Intruder missions over Luftwaffe bomber airfields.

22/23 & 23/24 December The 'Manchester Blitz'.

29/30 December The 'Second Great Fire of London' devastates the City.

1941
2/3 January The CAI makes a last appearance over the UK.

January Ground Control Interception (GCI) instituted.

February The first 'Domino' station, intended to jam *Y-Gerät*, begins operating.

6 February In Führer Directive No 23, Hitler orders the Luftwaffe to concentrate on ports and merchant shipping.

3/4 & 4/5 March The 'Cardiff Blitz'.

12/13 March Heavy attack on Merseyside. The defences make a breakthrough, with night fighters claiming five bombers.

13/14 & 14/15 March The 'Clydeside Blitz'.

19/20 March The heaviest attack of the Blitz so far is made on London.

March & April Luftwaffe Kampfgruppen are withdrawn from western Europe for the campaign in the Balkans.

15/16 April & 4/5 May The 'Belfast Blitz'.

16/17 & 19/20 April Massive attacks are made on London, dwarfing all that came before. The second raid is the heaviest of the entire Blitz.

21–23 & 28–29 April The 'Plymouth Blitz'. The Devonport naval base and town are badly damaged.

26/27 April, 2/3, 3/4 & 7/8 May The 'Mersey Blitz'.

5/6 & 6/7 May The 'Greenock Blitz'.

10/11 May Luftwaffe makes a final attack on London. By the end of the month, the whole of Luftflotte 2 has been withdrawn in preparation for *Barbarossa*.

ATTACKER'S CAPABILITIES
The Luftwaffe in its prime

In 1940, the Luftwaffe, despite the losses suffered since May, was arguably the best all-round air force in the world. The forthcoming campaign would be fought by well-trained crews, equipped with world-leading navigation equipment. Conversely, no air force had embarked upon a strategic air offensive of this kind before 1940 and the doctrine developed by the Luftwaffe had not envisaged a campaign of this magnitude.

Doctrine

Giulio Douhet's work gained considerable attention in some inter-war air forces, notably those of Britain and the United States. Both were primarily maritime powers and both had been dragged unwillingly into fighting on the Western Front in World War I. The attraction of a fleet of bombers, able to attack and destroy an enemy's capability for making war, as well as civilian morale, was obvious. In Germany, however, attitudes were more divided. One school of thought promoted the concept of 'Total War', in which the industrial capacity of a nation was a legitimate target. This included not only the factory but the worker and his home. In 1926, the *Truppenamt Luftschutzreferat* (Army Troop Bureau, Air Defence Desk) published *Richtlinien für die Führungs des operative Luftkrieges* (Directives for the Conduct of the Operational Air War). The author, Oberstleutnant Helmut Wilberg, foresaw a future in which a new German air force performed a dual role. The first was to support the *Heer* (the German Army) with a tactical air force. The second was to attack the enemy homeland, targeting industry and civilian morale.

As early as 1932, the requirement for a Uralbomber had been issued, calling for an aircraft with sufficient range to strike targets deep in Russia – or Scapa Flow in the north of Scotland. The revised specification called for 1,600kg (3,527lb) of bombs to be carried 2,000km (1,243 miles). Two contenders, the Dornier Do 19 and Junkers Ju 89, flew at the end of 1936. The engines of neither aircraft were supercharged and their performance was

The Dornier Do 17 began life as a 'mail plane' but soon entered Luftwaffe service as a reconnaissance aircraft and fast bomber.
By the autumn of 1940, the Do 17Z was in the process of replacement by the Junkers Ju 88. (ullstein bild/Contributor, Getty)

predictably disappointing. Nazi propaganda demanded large numbers of aircraft and the German economy was simply not strong enough to build large fleets of both twin and four-engine bombers. Göring, told that two and a half twin-engine bombers could be produced for the same amount of aluminium as one four-engine aircraft, is alleged to have asserted that the Führer did not ask how big the Luftwaffe's bombers were but how many there were. The Uralbomber programme was cancelled in 1937 but, even before the prototypes flew, the far-sighted Chief of Staff, Generalleutnant Walther Wever, had ordered a new design study: 'Bomber A'. This eventually resulted in the flawed Heinkel He 177.

Luftwaffe order of battle, bomber and long-range reconnaissance units, 7 September 1940					
Unit	Equipment	Strength	Serviceable	Base	Name
Luftflotte 2 (Brussels, Generalfeldmarschall Albert Kesselring)					
1.(F)/Aufklärungsgruppe 22	Do 17, Bf 110	13	9	Lille	
2.(F)/Aufklärungsgruppe 122	Ju 88, He 111	10	9	Brussels/Melsbroek	
4.(F)/Aufklärungsgruppe 122	Ju 88, He 111, Bf 110	13	9	Brussels	
I Fliegerkorps (Beauvais, Generaloberst Ulrich Grauert)					
5.(F)/Aufklärungsgruppe 122	Ju 88, He 111	11	11	Haute-Fontaine	
Stab/KG 76	Do 17	6	3	Cormeilles-en-Vexin	
I/KG 76	Do 17	26	19	Beauvais/Tille	
II/KG 76	Ju 88	27	21	Creil	
III/KG 76	Do 17	24	17	Cormeilles-en-Vexin	
Stab/KG 77	Ju 88	1	1	Laon	
I/KG 77	Ju 88	36	31	Laon	
II/KG 77	Ju 88	32	25	Asch-Nord	
III/KG 77	Ju 88	30	19	Laon	
Stab/KG 1	He 111	7	5	Rosiéres-en-Santerre	*Hindenburg*
I/KG 1	He 111	36	22	Montdidier and Clairmont	*Hindenburg*
II/KG 1	He 111	36	23	Montdidier and Nijmegen	*Hindenburg*
III/KG 1	Ju 88	9	0	Rosiéres-en-Santerre	*Hindenburg*
Stab/KG 30	Ju 88	1	1	Brussels	
I/KG 30	Ju 88	10	1	Brussels	
II/KG 30	Ju 88	30	24	Gilze-Rijen	
Stab/KG 26	He 111	6	3	Gilze-Rijen	*Löwen*
I/KG 26	He 111	25	7	Moerbeke and Courtrai	*Löwen*
II/KG 26	He 111	26	7	Gilze-Rijen	*Löwen*
II Fliegerkorps (Ghent, General Bruno Lörzer)					
1.(F)/Aufklärungsgruppe 122	Ju 88	5	3	Holland	
7.(F)/LG 2	Bf 110	14	9	Unknown	
Stab/KG 2	Do 17	6	6	Saint-Léger	*Holzhammer*
I/KG 2	Do 17	19	12	Cambrai	*Holzhammer*
II/KG 2	Do 17	31	20	Saint-Léger	*Holzhammer*
III/KG 2	Do 17	30	30	Cambrai	*Holzhammer*
Stab/KG 53	He 111	5	3	Lille	*Legion Condor*
I/KG 53	He 111	23	19	Lille	*Legion Condor*
II/KG 53	He 111	29	7	Lille	*Legion Condor*

Luftwaffe order of battle, bomber and long-range reconnaissance units, 7 September 1940					
III/KG 53	He 111	19	4	Lille	*Legion Condor*
Stab/KG 3	Do 17	6	5	Le Culot	*Blitz*
I/KG 3	Do 17	29	25	Le Culot	*Blitz*
II/KG 3	Do 17	27	23	Antwerp/Deurne	*Blitz*
III/KG 3	Do 17	28	19	Saint-Trond	*Blitz*
Erprobungsgruppe 210	Bf 110, Bf 109	26	17	Denain/Valenciennes	
IX Fliegerdivision (IX Fliegerkorps from 16 October 1940) (Soesterberg, Generalleutnant Joachim Coeler)					
3.(F)/Aufklärungsgruppe 122	Ju 88, He 111	11	10	Eindhoven	
Stab/KG 4	He 111	5	5	Soesterberg	*General Wever*
I/KG 4	He 111	37	16	Soesterberg	*General Wever*
II/KG 4	He 111	37	30	Eindhoven	*General Wever*
III/KG 4	Ju 88	30	14	Amsterdam/Schiphol	*General Wever*
Kampfgruppe 126	He 111	33	26	Nantes	
Stab/KG 40	Ju 88	2	1	Bordeaux/Mérignac	
Küstenfliegergruppe 106	He 115, Do 18	28	16	Brittany and Borkum	
Luftflotte 3 (Saint-Cloud, Generalfeldmarschall Hugo Sperrle)					
1.(F)/Aufklärungsgruppe 123	Ju 88, Do 17	10	7	Paris	
2.(F)/Aufklärungsgruppe 123	Ju 88, Do 17	10	8	Paris	
3.(F)/Aufklärungsgruppe 123	Ju 88, Do 17	13	9	Paris/Buc	
IV Fliegerkorps (Sèvres with forward HQ at Dinard, General Kurt Pflugbeil)					
3.(F)/Aufklärungsgruppe 121	Do 17	10	6	NW France	
Stab/LG 1	Ju 88	3	3	Orléans/Bricy	
I/LG 1	Ju 88	27	13	Orléans/Bricy	
II/LG 1	Ju 88	31	19	Orléans/Bricy	
III/LG 1	Ju 88	30	19	Châteaudun	
Kampfgruppe 806	Ju 88	27	18	Nantes and Caen/Carpiquet	
Stab/KG 27	He 111	7	4	Tours	*Boelcke*
I/KG 27	He 111	35	13	Tours	*Boelcke*
II/KG 27	He 111	32	15	Dinard and Bourges	*Boelcke*
III/KG 27	He 111	20	13	Rennes/Saint-Jacques	*Boelcke*
Kampfgruppe 100	He 111	28	7	Vannes/Meucon	*Wiking*
Kampfgruppe 606	Do 17	33	29	Brest/Lanvéoc-Poulmic and Cherbourg	
3.(F)/Aufklärungsgruppe 31	Do 17, Bf 110	9	5	Saint-Brieuc	
I/KG 40	Fw 200	7	4	Bordeaux/Mérignac	
V Fliegerkorps (Villacoublay, General Ritter von Greim)					
4.(F)/Aufklärungsgruppe 121	Ju 88, Do 17	13	5	Normandy	
4.(F)/Aufklärungsgruppe 14	Bf 110, Do 17	12	9	Normandy	

Luftwaffe order of battle, bomber and long-range reconnaissance units, 7 September 1940					
Stab/KG 51	Ju 88	1	0	Orly	*Edelweiss*
I/KG 51	Ju 88	33	13	Melun/Villaroche	*Edelweiss*
II/KG 51	Ju 88	34	17	Orly	*Edelweiss*
III/KG 51	Ju 88	34	27	Étampes	*Edelweiss*
Stab/KG 54	Ju 88	1	0	Évreux	*Totenkopf*
I/KG 54	Ju 88	30	18	Évreux	*Totenkopf*
II/KG 54	Ju 88	26	14	St. André-de-l'Eure	*Totenkopf*
Stab/KG 55	He 111	6	6	Villacoublay	*Greif*
I/KG 55	He 111	27	20	Dreux	*Greif*
II/KG 55	He 111	30	22	Chartres	*Greif*
III/KG 55	He 111	25	20	Villacoublay	*Greif*
Luftflotte 5 (Kristiansund, Generaloberst Hans-Jürgen Stumpff)					
X Fliegerkorps (Stavanger, General Hans Geisler)					
2.(F)/Aufklärungsgruppe 22	Do 17	9	5	Stavanger	
3.(F)/Aufklärungsgruppe 22	Do 17	9	5	Stavanger	
1.(F)/Aufklärungsgruppe 120	He 111, Ju 88	13	2	Stavanger	
1.(F)/Aufklärungsgruppe 121	He 111, Ju 88	7	2	Stavanger and Aalborg	
1/Küstenfliegergruppe 506	He 115	8	6	Stavanger	
2/Küstenfliegergruppe 506	He 115	5	5	Trondheim and Tromsø	
3/Küstenfliegergruppe 506	He 115	8	6	List	
	Totals	1,558	981		
Corpo Aereo Italiano order of battle, bomber units, 22 October 1940					
Gruppo	Squadriglie	Equipment	Strength	Base	
11	1 & 4	Fiat BR 20	19	Melsbroek	
43	3 & 5	Fiat BR 20	19	Melsbroek	
98	240 & 241	Fiat BR 20	19	Chièvres	
99	242 & 243	Fiat BR 20	18	Chièvres	

The thinking espoused by Wilberg and Wever was summarized in the Luftwaffe's official doctrinal document, *Luftwaffe Dienstvorschrift 16: Luftkriegführung* (Luftwaffe Service Regulation 16: Air War Guidance or LDv 16). This dismissed the Douhetian idea of targeting civilian morale. Instead, the Luftwaffe would support the *Heer*, while remaining capable of undertaking 'strategic' operations against a range of industrial, economic and government targets should the circumstances call for them. The Legion Condor's experience in Spain essentially confirmed the Luftwaffe's doctrinal thinking. The results from the Legion's few 'strategic' missions were mixed and it was clear that bombing accuracy needed improvement.

Although no stranger to the concept of a strategic air campaign, the organization of the Luftwaffe was based on individual *Luftflotten* (Air Fleets). These, with their own complements of bomber, fighter and reconnaissance units were, operationally speaking, very flexible and designed to support army formations in the field. Orders issued by the *Oberkommando der Luftwaffe* (OKL) *Generalstab* (General Staff) were tied to the requirements of the *Heer* and detailed planning was undertaken by the individual Luftflotten and their own Fliegerkorps. This worked brilliantly in 1939 and 1940, but emerged as a built-in weakness when the time came to formulate a coherent strategic campaign against Britain.

The Heinkel He 111 was 'blooded' in the Spanish Civil War. Although no longer the most modern of bombers by the Blitz, the He 111 continued to form the backbone of the *Kampfwaffe* throughout the campaign. (ullstein bild/Contributor, Getty)

Wever's death in an air accident in 1937 extinguished one of the Luftwaffe's leading lights. It did not, however, stop the protracted development of the He 177. Albert Kesselring, Wever's successor as Chief of Staff, remained confident that the new twin-engine bombers then entering service could undertake a strategic campaign – should one be needed.

The aircraft

Kesselring's belief stemmed from the performance offered by a new, fast bomber which appeared in 1937. The specification for what became the Heinkel He 111 was issued at the same time as that of the Uralbomber. Although the first incarnation of the He 111 was an airliner, its real purpose as a tactical medium bomber was soon revealed by the He 111B. This boasted a top speed of 230mph and a maximum range of 1,030 miles with a 1,653lb bombload. The He 111 saw action over Spain, where its relatively high speed offset a light defensive armament.

Substantial revisions were made to the design, and the familiar cigar-shaped He 111H and P-series aircraft were in service for the campaigns of 1939–41. By this stage, the drag-inducing 'dustbin' ventral gun position had been discarded. A streamlined gondola took its place, unflatteringly known by some crews as the '*Sterbebett*' or 'Deathbed'. Modern fighter opposition revealed the He 111's shortcomings in both speed and defensive armament during the western campaigns. By the summer of 1940, the aircraft was being gradually withdrawn in favour of the Ju 88. Nevertheless, the Heinkel remained the backbone of the Luftwaffe's bomber force at the beginning of the Blitz. In September 1940, three Kampfgeschwader were fully equipped with the He 111, in addition to two Kampfgruppen. Three more He 111 Kampfgeschwader were in the process of transferring to the Ju 88.

The Junkers Ju 88 *Schnellbomber* was easily the most modern and capable bomber in the Luftwaffe's inventory. Service versions were considerably heavier than the prototypes but the aircraft possessed almost fighter-like speed and manoeuvrability. The Ju 88 could outrun the Blenheim night fighter. (PhotoQuest/Contributor, Getty)

The Dornier Do 17, nicknamed the 'Flying Pencil' by virtue of its slim fuselage, first flew as a supposed civil airliner and mail carrier in 1934. It was a failure in that role, which is scarcely

OPPOSITE LUFTWAFFE DEPLOYMENT, 7 SEPTEMBER 1940

surprising, as the aircraft was in fact designed from the outset as a fast twin-engine bomber. The aircraft entered Luftwaffe service as the Do 17E bomber and Do 17F reconnaissance aircraft. In common with other Luftwaffe contemporaries, the Dornier saw combat over Spain and crews quickly came to appreciate its speed and pleasant handling characteristics.

At the end of 1938, the Do 17Z entered service, which incorporated the lessons learned in Spain. A distinctive enlarged forward fuselage enhanced visibility, and defensive armament was improved. The aircraft suffered a high loss rate over France and Britain where, in common with the He 111, a relatively low speed and poor armament left it unable to cope with modern opposition. Production had ended by September 1940, when only two Kampfgeschwader were still fully equipped with the Do 17, while a third was converting to the Ju 88. The Dornier's short range and light bombload did not make it well suited to the forthcoming campaign and it was the least effective of the Luftwaffe's three bombers.

In the spring of 1935, the *Technische Amt* (Technical Directorate) of the *Reichsluftministerium* (National Air Ministry or RLM) issued an ambitious requirement for a *Schnellbomber* (fast bomber) to complement and then replace the existing generation of bombers. The specification called for a maximum bombload of 1,765lb and a top speed of 310mph – well in advance of types such as the Martin B-10 or Vickers Wellington. The design submitted by Junkers, the Ju 88, made use of stressed-skin construction, which imparted greater lightness and strength over previous techniques. When the Junkers' rival designs fell by the wayside, the Luftwaffe lost no time in ordering the Ju 88 into mass production. By this stage, a dive-bombing capability had been added to the aircraft and weight increased accordingly. The first examples entered service in March 1939. A further redesign, in which the wingspan was increased, resulted in the Ju 88A-4 and A-5 (although the latter actually preceded the A-4 on the production line).

Despite the added weight and some tricky handling qualities, the lively performance of the Ju 88 endeared it to its crews. The aircraft could lift a heavier bombload further and faster than either the He 111 or Do 17, making it the most formidable of the trio. At the time of the Blitz, the Ju 88 equipped four complete Kampfgeschwadern and five more units were in the process of conversion. In addition, the type was operated by 11 of the Aufklärungsgruppen (Reconnaissance Groups) in the west.

Luftwaffe medium bomber performance			
Aircraft	Maximum speed (loaded)	Maximum range	Normal bombload
Heinkel He 111P-4	200mph (322km/h)	1,490 miles (2,398km) (with overload fuel)	4,408lb (2,000kg)
Dornier Do 17Z-2	224mph (360km/h)	720 miles (1,159km)	2,205lb (1,000kg)
Junkers Ju 88A-4	292mph (470km/h)	1,696 miles (2,729km)	4,420lb (2,005kg) (maximum)

Equipment and tactics

One of the lesser-known lessons the Legion Condor drew from its experience in Spain was the problem of target-finding in darkness and poor weather. Accordingly, much effort was put into developing effective navigation aids in the years leading up to the outbreak of war. When Luftflotten 2 and 3 moved into their new airfields in the summer of 1940, much of the preparation for the campaign against Britain in 1940 focused on building a comprehensive ground-based navigation system. These aids can be divided into three broad categories: blind landing, navigation and bomb-aiming.

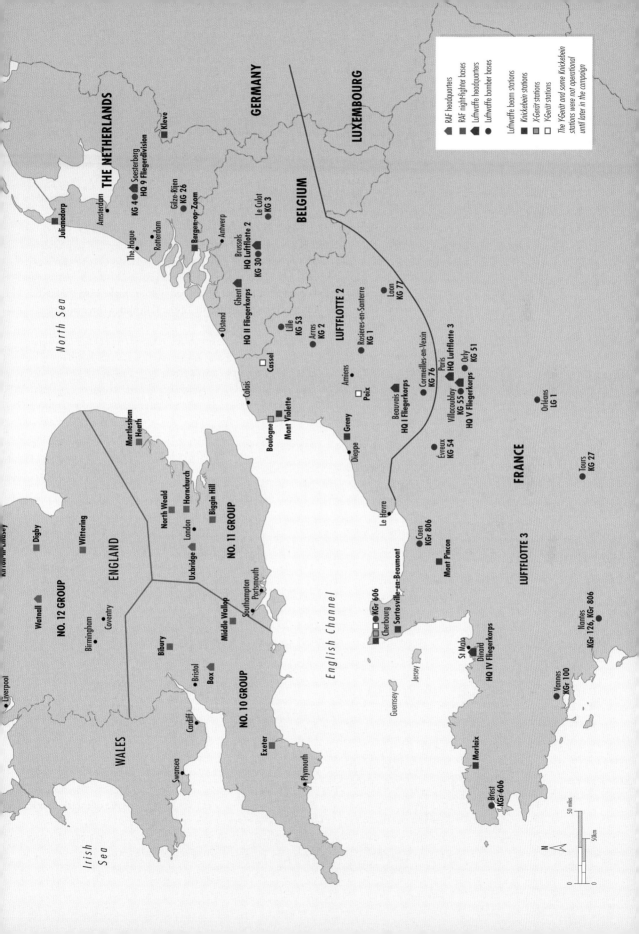

Legend:

RAF headquarters
RAF night-fighter bases
Luftwaffe headquarters
Luftwaffe bomber bases

Luftwaffe beam stations
Knickebein stations
X-Gerät stations
Y-Gerät stations

The X-Gerät and some Knickebein stations were not operational until later in the campaign

North Sea

THE NETHERLANDS

GERMANY

LUXEMBOURG

BELGIUM

Amsterdam
Juliumodorp
The Hague
Rotterdam
KG 4 Soesterberg HQ 9 Fliegerdivision
Kleve
Gilze-Rijen KG 26
Bergen-op-Zoom
Le Culot KG 3
Antwerp
Brussels HQ Luftflotte 2
KG 30
Ghent HQ II Fliegerkorps
Ostend
Lille KG 53
Arras KG 2
Rosieres-en-Santerre KG 1
Laon KG 77
LUFTFLOTTE 2
Cassel
Calais
Mont Violette
Amiens
Poix
Cormeilles-en-Vexin KG 76
Paris HQ Luftflotte 3
Orly KG 51
Villacoublay KG 55 HQ V Fliegerkorps
Beauvais HQ I Fliegerkorps
Boulogne
Greny
Dieppe
Le Havre
Évreux KG 54
Orléans LG 1
Tours KG 27
FRANCE
LUFTFLOTTE 3

North Sea

Liverpool
Kirton-in-Lindsey
Digby
Wittering
Watnall
NO. 12 GROUP
Birmingham
Coventry
Bibury
Bristol
Box
WALES
Cardiff
Swansea
Exeter
Plymouth
ENGLAND
Martlesham Heath
North Weald
Hornchurch
London Uxbridge
Biggin Hill
NO. 11 GROUP
Southampton
Portsmouth
Middle Wallop
NO. 10 GROUP

English Channel

Guernsey
Jersey

KGr 806 Caen
Sortosville-en-Beaumont
KGr 606 Cherbourg
Mont Pincon
St Malo
Dinard HQ IV Fliegerkorps
Vannes KGr 100
Nantes KGr 126, KGr 806
Morlaix
Brest I,KGr 606

Irish Sea

N

50 miles
50km

OPPOSITE *X-GERÄT* DIAGRAM OF ATTACK ON CASTLE BROMWICH

On the night of 13/14 August 1940, He 111s of KGr 100 attacked the Spitfire Shadow Factory at Castle Bromwich. The factory complex was hit by 11 bombs – a high degree of accuracy. The raid proved to Air Intelligence that the Luftwaffe had a bombing system well in advance of anything then possessed by the RAF.

Lorenz

In the late 1920s and early 1930s, attempts by European airlines to maintain regular schedules were made impossible by adverse weather. C. Lorenz AG of Berlin developed a blind-landing system, able to guide aircraft to all but the most fog-shrouded airfields. The system employed two adjacent transmitters, which emitted a pair of beams up to a range of 30 miles. The left-hand beam was made of Morse dots, the right-hand beam of Morse dashes. The two beams overlapped in the middle, where the dots and dashes merged to form a continuous note or equisignal. When the steady note was heard, the listener knew his aircraft was on course for the runway. By the mid-1930s, the system had revolutionized commercial flying, for airline services could adhere to a published timetable, despite the vagaries of the weather. It was also employed by the RAF – and the bomber units of the nascent Luftwaffe.

Knickebein

Telefunken, a German rival to the Lorenz company, produced a relatively simple method of marking targets with a pair of radio beams. One beam guided the aircraft to the target, in much the same way as an ordinary Lorenz beam. A second beam crossed the first over the bomb-release point.

The system was given the name *Knickebein* ('Crooked Leg'), which was either an allusion to the cross beam itself or to a mythical raven of Norse legend. More importantly, *Knickebein* offered two particular advantages: it used the same Lorenz equipment found in all German bombers and worked on the same frequencies (30, 31.5 and 33.3 MHz). Secondly, any crewmember trained in the use of the Lorenz-blind approach system could use *Knickebein*. In other words, it was a bomb-aiming system that could be used by the entire Luftwaffe bomber force.

The *Knickebein* relied on large ground transmitters, the aerial arrays of which were 100ft tall and 315ft wide. These rested on curved rails, enabling the beam to be aligned on the desired target. The range of the system was dependent on the receiving aircraft's altitude: a bomber flying at 20,000ft could receive the *Knickebein* signals 270 miles away – but, in practice, few of the Luftwaffe's bombers reached or exceeded that height in 1940.

Knickebein's main disadvantage was that the 'steady note' lane of the approach beam was one-third of a degree in width. Therefore, the width of the beam was one mile at a range of 180 miles. This was not good enough for accurate bombing of most British towns and cities by night. As the Blitz went on and RAF countermeasures became more effective, many crews used *Knickebein* simply as a guide to a target's vicinity, after which bombing was done visually.

The *X-Gerät*

In early 1934, the Deputy Minister of Aviation Erhard Milch asked Dr Hans Plendl, a radio wave expert, to begin work

Heinkel He 111s of Kampfgruppe 100, probably photographed prior to the Blitz. KGr 100 began the campaign as the Luftwaffe's primary target-marking unit but generally poor results meant the unit's status was gradually eroded as the Blitz wore on. The unit emblem of a Norse Longship is visible on the nose of the nearest aircraft. (Air Historical Branch: Ken Wakefield Collection)

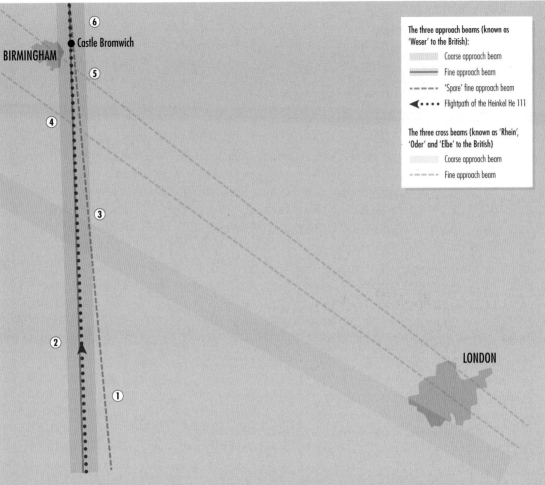

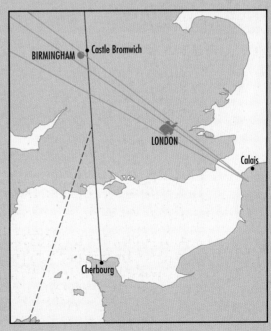

The three approach beams (known as 'Weser' to the British):

Coarse approach beam

Fine approach beam

'Spare' fine approach beam

Flightpath of the Heinkel He 111

The three cross beams (known as 'Rhein', 'Oder' and 'Elbe' to the British)

Coarse approach beam

Fine approach beam

Map points and associated commentary:

1. X-Gerät used six beams, emitted from ground stations in German-held territory. Three of these beams, two fine and one coarse, were directed straight at the target. Three cross beams intersected the approach beams at various distances from the target.

2. A KGr 100 crew first located the coarse approach beam. The aircraft then settled on to the very narrow fine beam contained within the coarse beam. A second fine approach beam was transmitted in case of technical malfunction. X-Gerät provided the pilot and observer with audio and visual means of staying accurately 'on the beam'.

3. When 50km (30 miles) from the aiming-point, the bomber flew through a first, coarse cross beam. This warned the crew that the aircraft must be aligned correctly in the approach beam.

4. When 20km (12 miles) from the bomb-release point, the aircraft flew through the second cross beam. At this point, in order to find the bomber's true groundspeed, the operator started the first hand on a special clock.

5. As the bomber flew through the third cross beam, so the first hand on the clock was stopped and a second hand started. This began the countdown to the target. As the distance from the second to the third cross beam (15km) was three times that between the third beam and the bomb release point (5km), so the second clock hand rotated three times faster than the first.

6. When the two hands came together, they closed a pair of electrical contacts which released the aircraft's bombs, theoretically on target.

on a blind-bombing system. The result was the *X-Gerät* (X-Device) which, while a good deal more complex than *Knickebein*, was the most advanced system of its type in the world when it entered service.

The *X-Gerät* system promised a high degree of accuracy, whatever the weather or time of day. The equipment required a high degree of skill to be used properly. The pilot had to maintain a constant speed, bearing and altitude on the bomb run. Wind speed had to be accurately assessed to allow for 'drift'. In 1938, a special unit using the cover name of the *Flugfunkerschule und Versuchskommando* (Radio Operators' Training and Experimental Command) was formed. In November 1939, the unit adopted the title of Kampfgruppe (KGr) 100 (*Wiking*) and the following month, an aircraft of the unit flew to London and back on a proving mission. The He 111s of KGr 100 (later KG 100) could be distinguished by the three dorsal antennae for the *X-Gerät* and the unit badge of a Viking longship on the forward fuselage.

The *Y-Gerät*

The redoubtable Dr Plendl was responsible for a third and even more sophisticated bomb-aiming device, which employed a single beam. In this, the beam's signals were received by the aircraft and returned by a transponder to the beam station. The radar method of calculating an aircraft's range (using the equation: distance = speed x time) established the bomber's distance from the station and therefore the distance to the target. When the aircraft reached the bomb-release point, the station sent a signal and the bombs were dropped. When the British Air Ministry discovered that the new system was known as *Woden* (Wotan), the one-eyed Norse God, it was surmised that the *Y-Gerät* used a single beam. In fact, this was pure coincidence, as *X-Gerät* was *Woden I* and *Y-Gerät* was *Woden II*. *Y-Gerät* was fitted to the He 111s of III/KG 26, which began intensive operations with the new equipment at the end of 1940.

The three systems offered the Luftwaffe a potential force-multiplier, allowing targets to be attacked with a good degree of accuracy in darkness and in all weathers. On the other hand, as the campaign went on, a variety of factors emerged which combined to blunt the advantage offered.

In addition, by the autumn of 1940 the Luftwaffe possessed a comprehensive network of radio beacons, which enabled bomber crews to determine their position through radio direction-finding 'fixes'. These were backed up by illuminated, visual beacons at all the Luftwaffe's airfields. Together, they were intended to do everything possible to ensure the safety of the Kampfflieger during the upcoming night offensive. Despite these measures, take-off and landing accidents did increase from September 1940 onwards. Available figures suggest that the Luftwaffe suffered more flying accidents than combat losses for much of the Blitz. Even Werner Baumbach, an experienced airman serving with KG 30, twice crashed in poor visibility on 16 October and 24 November.

Target-marking methods

Although the electronic equipment used by the Luftwaffe was world-leading, the methods of target-marking were crude and largely ineffective. The units which specialized in target-marking, KGr 100, III/KG 26 and II/KG 55, relied on the *Fallschirmleuchtbombe* LC 50F (parachute illumination bomb) and the B1E1 1kg incendiary. These lightweight weapons had a tendency to drift in the wind after they were dropped, sometimes for a considerable distance. Therefore, no matter how accurate the marking, the subsequent aiming-point for the rest of the bombers could be wrong by hundreds of yards. A pathfinder unit could be active for an hour or more over a town but 'back-up' marking – the continual re-marking of a target during a raid – was not formally practised. Once the specialist target-markers had opened the attack, the main force would continue the bombing, often for hours. The original markers burned out, were extinguished or became lost in the fires started by other bombers.

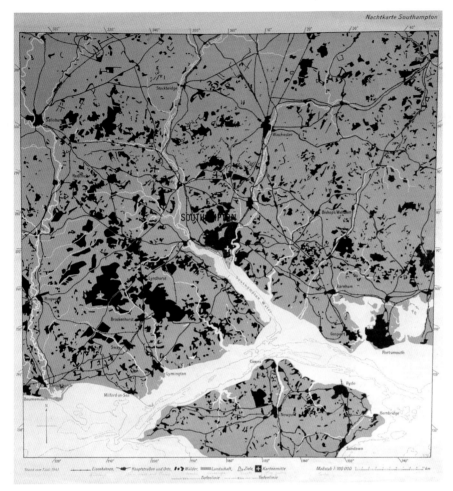

Nachtkarte Southampton

A *Nachtkarte* map of Southampton. The maps were intended for use under cockpit lighting. The target areas – Southampton's docks – are coloured yellow. The roads, railways and woods are clearly delineated to assist navigation. (Royal Geographical Society/Contributor, Getty)

The method of attacking targets in darkness ranged from individual *Störangriffen* (nuisance attacks) by single aircraft, to mass raids by several hundred aircraft. From the outset of the Blitz, the technique most frequently adopted was a continuous attack on a target over a long time period, perhaps eight or nine hours, or as long as the darkness lasted. At other times, the distance to a target or deteriorating weather forced attacks to be concentrated in time, perhaps lasting less than two hours. The incoming and outgoing flightpaths could be from several directions, as units based across France, Belgium, the Netherlands and Denmark converged on a target. Airfield control dispatched the bombers at intervals of about four minutes and the aircraft flew in a stream, or *Krokodil*, at various heights and at approximately 19km (12-mile) intervals.

Anti-shipping capability

The campaign against shipping, through minelaying or by attacks on ships at sea or in harbour, was a key part of the Luftwaffe's blockade strategy. Unfortunately, the rivalry between the Luftwaffe and the *Kriegsmarine* (Nazi Germany's navy) meant that cooperation between the two was perfunctory at best.

The aerial minelaying campaign was compromised from an early stage by the British discovery of a magnetic mine on the Thames mudflats in November 1939. The Luftwaffe's main anti-shipping capability was vested in Generalleutnant Hans Geisler's Fliegerkorps X, based in Norway and Denmark. This command was required to hand over some of its units

The Luftwaffe's long-range anti-shipping capability was vested in the heavily armed Focke-Wulf Fw 200 Condor. This converted airliner was capable of flying far out into the Atlantic, reporting and attacking British convoys. (Popperfoto/ Contributor, Getty)

to Kesselring's Luftflotte 2 during August 1940, when the economic blockade was subordinated to the bid for air superiority.

The long-range maritime patrol Fw 200 Condor entered service with KG 40 in October 1939, originally intended as a stop gap before the appearance of the He 177 in the anti-shipping role. Other units specializing in maritime operations (mostly minelaying) flew the He 111 or the Ju 88. These included I and II/KG 26, KG 30, and Kampfgruppen 126, 606 and 806. For much of the Blitz, these units were distributed among three separate Fliegerkorps and most of their work entailed attacks on land targets.

Defensive tactics

For Luftwaffe bomber crews, the best way to survive a night-fighter attack was by spotting the assailant before it had time to close within range. Some crews flew just below the cloud base, which gave an immediate refuge if attacked. Of the three bombers, the Ju 88 offered the best chance of escape. Pilot Officer Roland Beamont, on a night patrol in an 87 Sqn Hurricane over Bristol in September 1940, gave chase to a Ju 88 which entered a dive and drew away into the darkness. Another method, which exploited the Ju 88's manoeuvrability, was for the pilot to throw the bomber into a steep left or right half-roll, then let the aircraft 'fall' on one wing – or even upside down – for some 2,000m (6,560ft), before levelling out and, if necessary, repeating the manoeuvre.

Weapons

The Zeiss-Jena Lotfe C/7D tachometric bombsight which equipped the three medium bombers in 1940 could, in ideal conditions, land 50 per cent of bombs within 91m (300ft) of a target from an altitude of 3,000m (9,842ft). At double this altitude (6,000m or 19,685ft), the error more than quadrupled, to 400m (1,300ft). In poor visibility, bombing error increased by another 250 per cent. As a rule of thumb, the average 'miss' distance on a training range is multiplied three fold when a bomb-aimer is operating in a war environment and under fire. To counter this inevitable inaccuracy, the sight's bomb release could be pre-set to intervals of 10–100m (33–330ft). If an aircraft was carrying 20 SC 50 bombs, the 'stick' could vary in length from 200m (660ft) to almost 2km (1.2 miles).

The Luftwaffe deployed four main categories of bomb during the Blitz. The high-explosive type used most frequently, especially in the early stages of the campaign, was the *Sprengbombe Cylindrisch* (SC or explosive bomb, cylindrical), which came in a variety of weights: 50kg, 250kg, 500kg and 1,000kg (the latter known as the Hermann for obvious reasons). Heavier, high-capacity versions (the SC 1200, SC 1800 'Satan', SC 2000 and SC 2500 'Max') were produced and dropped later in the campaign. Due to their effect on aircraft handling and performance, these weapons were dropped by specially trained crews.

From the middle of September, the high-capacity SB 1000 (*Spezialbombe* or *Luftmine*) began to be used. This was an anti-shipping mine adapted for use over land. They were known by the British as landmines, aerial mines or parachute mines. Originally designed to break a ship's keel, they were extremely powerful and, as they descended by parachute, impossible to aim with any accuracy.

The smallest bomb but undoubtedly the most destructive was the 1kg B1E1 *Elektronbrandbombe* (electron incendiary bomb), a weapon descended from those dropped by the Gothas in 1917–18. The bomb was filled with thermite explosive which ignited the electron magnesium alloy casing. The heat generated was enough to melt steel. Later, some were fitted with a small explosive charge, the purpose of which was either to blow a hole in a roof and allow the bomb to drop through, or to deter those trying to extinguish it. The bombs were packed in containers (the BSK *Schuttkasten* or cluster-bomb container) of 36 each. Several hundred B1E1s could be scattered over a target by a single aircraft.

Aircrew

In 1940, the Luftwaffe had in its ranks some of the best-trained airmen in the world. They were the fruit of an intensive instruction programme, in which quality was, for the most part, prioritized over quantity. From 1935, prospective Luftwaffe aircrew attended the following courses:

- An FEA (*Flieger-Ersatzabteilung*: Air Training Battalion) or FAR (*Flieger-Ausbildungsregiment*: Air Training Regiment) for six to 12 months of basic training.
- Aircrew then went on a two-month course at a *Fluganwärterkompanie* (Air Cadet Company). They then joined the *Fliegerführerschulen* (Pilot Schools) A/B at the FEA/FAR airfield for 100–150 hours of flying training.
- Bomber crew then went to a *Fliegerschule* (Air Training School) C for 60 hours of flying.
- A *Blindflugschule* (Instrument Training School) was attended for 50–60 hours of flying.
- Then three months were spent at a *Waffenschule* (Operational Training School) or other specialist school.
- Observers (*Beobachter*) were trained to fly to C standard, then spent nine to 12 months at *Aufklärungsfliegerschulen* (Reconnaissance Flying Schools) (which included instrument training).

The imposing figure of Reichsmarschall Hermann Göring. Although not as foolish as his reputation suggests, he was taken aback by the Luftwaffe's failure over Britain in August and September 1940. Thereafter, he took little interest in the campaign. (Alexander Binder/Stringer, Getty)

Pilots theoretically had at least 250 flying hours before joining their units. Corners were cut, however, so that the Luftwaffe could expand at the rate demanded. The *Beobachter* was trained to a level of reasonable proficiency in all the roles within a multi-engine aircraft. In terms of operational experience, the Luftwaffe possessed a cadre of airmen, some of whom had fought in Spain. Many more had flown in the campaigns in Poland, Scandinavia and the west.

Set against this, however, were the heavy losses sustained by the *Kampfwaffe* (bomber force) between May and September: 1,142 bombers were lost to all causes, representing 65 per cent of the force's initial strength prior to the invasion of France. By September 1940, the tempo of operations had dropped serviceability to less than two-thirds of the total strength as shown in the table.

Luftwaffe aircraft serviceability, 1940			
Date	Total strength	Serviceable aircraft	Serviceable aircraft as percentage of total strength
4 May 1940 (eve of western offensive)	1,758	1,180	67%
10 August 1940 (eve of *Adlertag*)	1,542	1,015	66%
7 September 1940 (eve of the Blitz)	1,436	876	61%

These losses naturally affected morale, as the Battle of Britain ground on with seemingly no result. Although nocturnal sorties offered almost complete immunity from the British defences, they also presented their own dangers. In addition, bombers could become lost in the darkness, either through navigational errors, visual decoys or electronic interference. The Luftwaffe's Sea Rescue Service, the *Seenotdienst*, used an assortment of vessels and obsolete

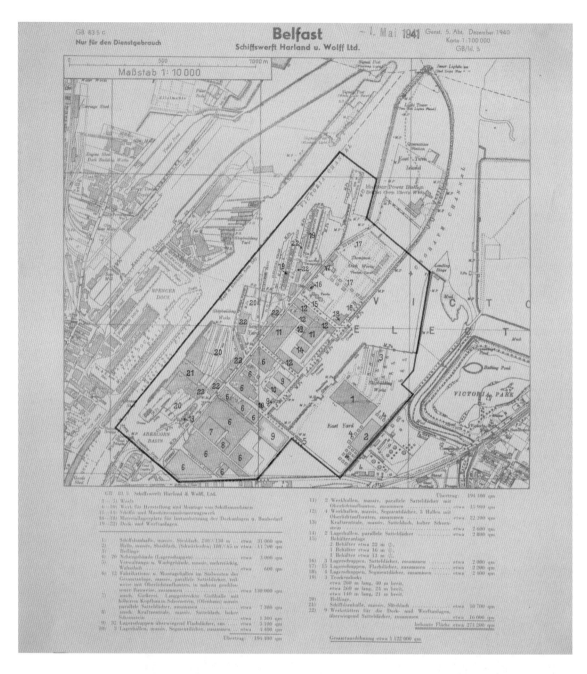

The Luftwaffe produced thousands of diligently compiled target folders, containing notes, maps and photographs. Not everything was accurate and by the Blitz, some information was out of date. This is the annotated map from the folder for the giant Harland & Wolff shipyards at Belfast.(IWM LBY LUFT 10)

Heinkel He 59 seaplanes to search for downed German (and British) airmen in the North Sea and English Channel.

Perhaps the greatest hazard to the German crews came from the weather. The Luftwaffe's *Orientierungsheft Grossbritannien* (Orientation Book Great Britain) provided details of British air defences, targets and meteorological conditions. A second volume gave a pessimistic but nevertheless accurate assessment of the expected climactic conditions: 'All in all, it appears that the British Isles, particularly in the winter months of frequent storms, fog and dense cloud, present very difficult meteorological flying conditions, which without doubt belong among the most unpleasant to be found in any of those major countries regarded as civilized.'

Intelligence

A primary weakness was the Luftwaffe's lack of accurate intelligence on Britain. Many of the *Abwehr*'s (Intelligence service's) attempts to establish a spy network in Britain had ended in tragicomic failure. The *Luftwaffenführungsstab* (Luftwaffe General Staff) acquired an intelligence section, the 5th Abteilung, in June 1935. This was taken over in January 1938 by Oberst Joseph 'Beppo' ('Boy') Schmid. Just 38 years old, Schmid was a shrewd and ambitious 'old Nazi'. He had participated in the abortive Beer Hall Putsch and it was no secret that Schmid owed his position to his friendship with Göring. Despite this, his relatively lowly rank did not confer on him the status he or his department really needed. Adolf Galland later said that Schmid was a 'complete wash-out', while Erhard Milch more tactfully remarked that he 'trimmed his sails to the wind'. Schmid spoke no foreign languages, had no previous experience in intelligence work and was known to be a 'convivial' drinker. His staff, many of whom were reservists and civilians, were similarly ill-equipped for the work they were expected to undertake.

Without Erhard Milch, the Luftwaffe would not have been the force it was in 1940. Milch's organizational brilliance as State Secretary at the RLM formed the third element in the Luftwaffe's triumvirate, alongside Göring's political connections and Walther Wever's intellect. (Library of Congress/Contributor, Getty)

Substantial information on the British economy had been gathered in 1939 and 1940 by the 'England experts' in Group III of the 5th Abteilung. This was mainly achieved by purloining information from rival intelligence services in the Reich, foreign newspapers (although there was a dearth of foreign-language speakers in Schmid's department) and outdated pre-war publications. A vast number of detailed target folders was produced, covering all manner of potential targets, from airfields to gasworks, aircraft factories to steelworks, and everything in between. Each target folder contained:

- a 1:250,000 scale map to determine the aircraft approach route(s)
- information concerning the proximity of British airfields
- information concerning navigational aids, such as rivers, roads and railway lines
- a 1:5,000 scale map of the target itself
- in addition, there were notes on the importance of the target, the best time to attack, the most suitable types of bomb and the target's defences.

The target folders and the photographs and maps they contained could become outdated as defences changed, factories moved to other work or production was even relocated somewhere else. There was little appreciation of the importance of industrial dispersal or the 'shadow factory' scheme.

General Albert Kesselring in thoughtful mood in September 1940. 'Smiling Albert' had, rightly, cancelled the Uralbomber programme when Luftwaffe Chief of Staff in 1935. As commander of Luftflotte 2, he would play a junior role in the campaign after September 1940. (ullstein bild/Contributor, Getty)

The forbidding visage of General Hugo Sperrle. His command, Luftflotte 3, had begun a night campaign against Britain in August 1940 and would subsequently undertake the lion's share of the Blitz, especially against the southern and south-western ports. (PhotoQuest/Contributor, Getty)

Hundreds of reconnaissance sorties were made during the Battle of Britain and the Blitz but there were insufficient *Fernaufklärungsgruppen* (long-range reconnaissance groups) to produce adequate intelligence on the multitude of targets in the UK. Post-sortie reports by bomber crews, though often inaccurate, were nevertheless given credence by Luftwaffe Intelligence officers. Schmid, himself a political animal, was reluctant to pass unfavourable information to Göring and others. Instead of good intelligence acting as a 'force enabler', the relatively small quantity of information gathered and the low quality of its interpretation had the opposite effect on the Luftwaffe's decision-making process.

Commanders

'Vain', 'corrupt' and 'ambitious' are some of the adjectives used by historians to describe Hermann Göring. Yet the image of a drug-addled sybarite discounts the intelligence, forcefulness and occasional bursts of energy which serve to underline the contradictions inherent in his character.

Göring's rise within the Nazi Party is well known: his dashing reputation and aristocratic connections; his wounding in the 'Beer Hall Putsch' and subsequent morphine addiction; the tendency towards grandiloquence on the one hand and idleness on the other. In short, he was a politician with little interest in technical matters. His own preferred soubriquet, '*Der Eiserne*' ('The Iron Man'), contrasts with the nickname given to him by his colleagues: '*Der Dicke*' ('Fat Man' or 'Fatty').

In 1935, Göring became Commander in Chief of the Luftwaffe, where his political influence combined well with Milch's organizational skills and Wever's understanding of air power. Wever's death and the sidelining of Milch in favour of Ernst Udet soon led to the virtual abandonment of long-term industrial planning within the Luftwaffe. Göring began to lose favour with Hitler after Dunkirk and the Battle of Britain, where both were unimpressed and frustrated by the Luftwaffe's failures. Neither showed much interest in the ensuing campaign. The lack of strategic direction, or understanding of the Luftwaffe's capabilities, would become evident during the Blitz.

Göring was fortunate to stand at the head of a corps of efficient commanders. One of the most outstanding was Albert Kesselring. A Staff Officer during World War I, he remained in the Reichswehr after the armistice. He transferred to the air force in 1933 and served as Chief of the General Staff of the Luftwaffe for a brief period from mid-1936. Kesselring led Luftflotte 2 through the western campaigns and the Battle of Britain. His cheerful façade, which existed primarily to conceal a loveless marriage, caused him to be known as 'Smiling Albert'. He remained at heart a soldier and, although a brilliant staff officer, was not a believer in the idea of a strategic bombing campaign.

Hugo Sperrle was older than both Göring and Kesselring. An infantry officer, he transferred to the new air force in 1935 and briefly commanded the Legion Condor. Like his Luftwaffe contemporaries, Sperrle was not an ardent devotee of air power, nor was he noted for his military acumen. He did, however, bring considerable organizational skills to his post as commander of Luftflotte 3. Although Sperrle affected a monocle, he apparently regarded his numerous aristocratic colleagues with contempt and his abrasive personality endeared him to few. It is rare for a man's character to be so accurately reflected by his appearance and Hitler remarked that he liked to have Sperrle present at difficult meetings, as he was one of his 'most brutal-looking generals'.

The *Corpo Aereo Italiano*

Mention should be made of the Italian Regia Aeronautica component, the *Corpo Aereo Italiano* (CAI), which operated against the UK from bases in Belgium between October 1940 and January 1941. Mussolini's aircrews were unfamiliar with the winter weather in north-west Europe and unprepared for the violence of the air war in which they found themselves.

The Fiat BR 20 bomber carried a small bombload and was too slow and poorly armed to defend itself in daylight. The bombers relied on the protection offered by the Fiat CR 42 biplane fighters in the CAI's daylight operations against the UK. The BR 20 could be used to attack at night, though accuracy was doubtful. The CAI fielded eight BR 20 *squadriglie*, with a total strength of 75 aircraft.

Early daylight encounters with Fighter Command gave food for thought during October and November. Further desultory and ineffective CAI operations were flown, usually in darkness, against the coastal towns of Harwich and Ipswich until January 1941.

The 'Pact of Steel'. The German propaganda magazine *Signal* published this illustration of Fiat BR 20s and Ju 88s attacking Britain. Events proved Mussolini's men to be chronically under-prepared for the campaign. (SeM/ Contributor, Getty)

DEFENDER'S CAPABILITIES
Defending British shores

The image of searchlights criss-crossing the sky remains one of the most enduring symbols of the Blitz. In reality, without radar guidance, the searchlights were only rarely able to locate the Luftwaffe's bombers for the AA guns. (Hulton Archive/Stringer, Getty)

In Britain, memories of the airship and Gotha raids were kept alive by the dire predictions made by novelists, journalists and politicians during the inter-war period. Accordingly, from the mid-1930s, the government began to reorganize and improve Britain's 'passive' and 'active' defences. The country's passive defences aimed to minimize the damage to the population and the economy. Broadly, these were known until the early stages of the Blitz as Air Raid Precautions (ARP) and from 1941 as Civil Defence. The Air Raid Precautions Act came into force in 1938 and by September 1940 there was a host of measures designed to minimize the consequences of successful enemy bombing.

RAF Night-fighter units order of battle, 1 September 1940				
Unit	Equipment	Strength	Serviceable	Base
10 Group (Box, Air Vice-Marshal Sir Quintin Brand)				
87 Squadron	Hurricane	15	9	Exeter
604 Squadron	Blenheim	14	11	Middle Wallop
11 Group (Uxbridge, Air Vice-Marshal Sir Keith Park)				
25 Squadron	Blenheim	16	14	North Weald
600 Squadron	Blenheim	14	9	Hornchurch
Fighter Interception Unit	Blenheim/Beaufighter			Tangmere
12 Group (Watnall, Air Vice-Marshal Sir Trafford Leigh-Mallory)				
23 Squadron	Blenheim	17	11	Wittering
29 Squadron	Blenheim	14	10	Wellingore
264 Squadron	Defiant	15	8	Kirton-in-Lindsey
13 Group (Blakelaw, Air Vice-Marshal Sir Richard Saul)				
219 Squadron	Blenheim	13	8	Leeming
141 Squadron	Defiant	16	9	Turnhouse

Civil defence

Evacuation

Even before war was declared, a mass evacuation moved some 1.5 million children and adults to relative safety. The experience was not a universally happy one and by January 1940 about half of all children and nine out of ten mothers had returned to their old homes. When the Blitz began there was a second, smaller, wave of official and unofficial evacuations. In addition, the machinery of many government departments moved from London to a variety of smaller towns across the country. Another consequence was a zealously enforced blackout.

The early-warning system

The UK possessed a comprehensive civil early-warning system and it was frequently tested by the Luftwaffe's *Störangriffen* raids from July 1940 onwards. The warnings were passed directly from Fighter Command to local civilian headquarters. The air raid signals became a familiar feature of life to millions of Britons.

Air raid precautions

'Air Raid Precautions' covered a multitude of organizations. The Air Raid Wardens' Service was formed in 1937. Recruitment was voluntary and, while not initially especially popular, by September 1939, there were nearly 1.6 million men and women in the ARP. Warden posts were staffed by around five local wardens and each post was responsible for a small area (in London there were ten posts per square mile). The wardens had a variety of tasks, most notably enforcing the blackout, sounding the air raid warnings, ensuring people took shelter and reporting bomb damage and fires to the ARP headquarters in their town or borough. There were other ARP services including messengers (as telephone lines could be cut), First Aid parties, rescue detachments and ambulance drivers. Not least was the Women's Voluntary Service which provided 165,000 ARP workers, including nurses, drivers and wardens.

An ARP Post by Auxiliary Fireman Reginald Mills. The painting depicts calm efficiency: two of the three wardens are female. Each has a specific task. The observer on the left searches for incidents. On the right, the range and bearing of an incident is estimated. The warden in the centre reports the incident to the control room. (Michael Nicholson/Contributor, Getty)

Fire services

Britain's regular fire services were reinforced by the Auxiliary Fire Service (AFS). In 1938 and 1939, the number of firemen nationally rose from 5,000 to 75,000 – 85 per cent of whom were auxiliaries. The private citizen was also encouraged to do his or her bit, with buckets of sand especially useful in smothering the ubiquitous 1kg incendiary. The stirrup fire pump, originally intended to wash cars or spray foliage, cost just 12s 6d but would save countless lives and buildings during the winter and spring of 1940–41.

'UXB'

The main responsibility for bomb disposal in Britain was taken by the army's Royal Engineers. Naval parties took care of munitions which fell on naval shore establishments, as well as any unexploded parachute mines. RAF Bomb Disposal Squads dealt with unexploded munitions (UXBs) on RAF airfields as well as any bombs which remained in downed enemy aircraft. Prioritization of UXBs and the allocation of teams for their safe removal was made by the Commissioners of each Civil Defence Region.

OPPOSITE ROYAL AIR FORCE DEPLOYMENT, 7 SEPTEMBER 1940

The UXB services were soon overwhelmed and, by September, 3,759 bombs were waiting to be defused. Overall, 8.5 per cent of all bombs dropped during the Blitz are estimated to have been UXBs. The authorized number of Bomb Disposal Sections rose from 24 in May 1940 to 220 by September. The work of the Bomb Disposal Sections was, it need hardly be said, time-consuming and extremely hazardous. It was spring 1941 before the disposal units were able to defuse the latest types of German fuses. Nor was it only Luftwaffe munitions: unexploded anti-aircraft shells, Z Battery rockets and other 'friendly' missiles had likewise to be disarmed.

Shelters

The Munich Crisis accelerated the provision of public shelters. Calls for deep underground shelters for all city-dwellers were deflected by the government, for their construction would have been financially exorbitant and deprived other defence projects of funding. The building of public shelters was left to local authorities and, as a consequence, their quality and number varied greatly from one area to another. Some authorities left their preparations too late and found themselves in competition with each other for scarce resources. An alternative was for families to have their own shelters. The Anderson shelter was a small corrugated-steel structure, intended for small gardens or yards. One and a half million Andersons were provided between February and September 1939. In 1941, the Morrison shelter – essentially a steel table – was produced for installation inside homes.

Propaganda

All available means were used to sustain civilian morale during the Blitz. The Ministry of Home Security monitored public attitudes via daily and weekly reports, while the Ministry of Information used its considerable powers to mould the content of newspapers and BBC radio broadcasts. Their work was vital, for there was no means of stopping the bombing – or of knowing when it would end.

Intelligence

RAF Air Intelligence gleaned information from a variety of sources, including prisoner interrogations and radio traffic intercepted by the Y-Service. KGr 100 was based at Vannes in the south-west of Luftflotte 3's area and the airfield was one of the last to be linked to the headquarters in Paris. Wireless messages were therefore sent to and from Vannes in the Luftwaffe Enigma cipher. During 1940, the Government Code and Cipher School at Bletchley Park could, given time, decipher and read Luftwaffe Enigma messages. As KGr 100 led many of the night-time raids, Air Intelligence was occasionally able to ready its own countermeasures before raids crossed the coast. Another tactic was to find where the German beams were directed during the afternoon before a raid.

Electronic countermeasures (ECM)

Knickebein: the 'Headache' and the 'Aspirin'

In June 1940, an Anson of the RAF Wireless Interception Unit picked up *Knickebein* signals for the first time. This discovery, backed up by other scraps of evidence, clearly indicated the existence of a Luftwaffe blind-bombing system. After being briefed on the situation by Dr R.V. Jones of Air Intelligence, Churchill ordered the formation of a radio-jamming organization at the highest priority. By August, 80 Wing RAF, under the energetic

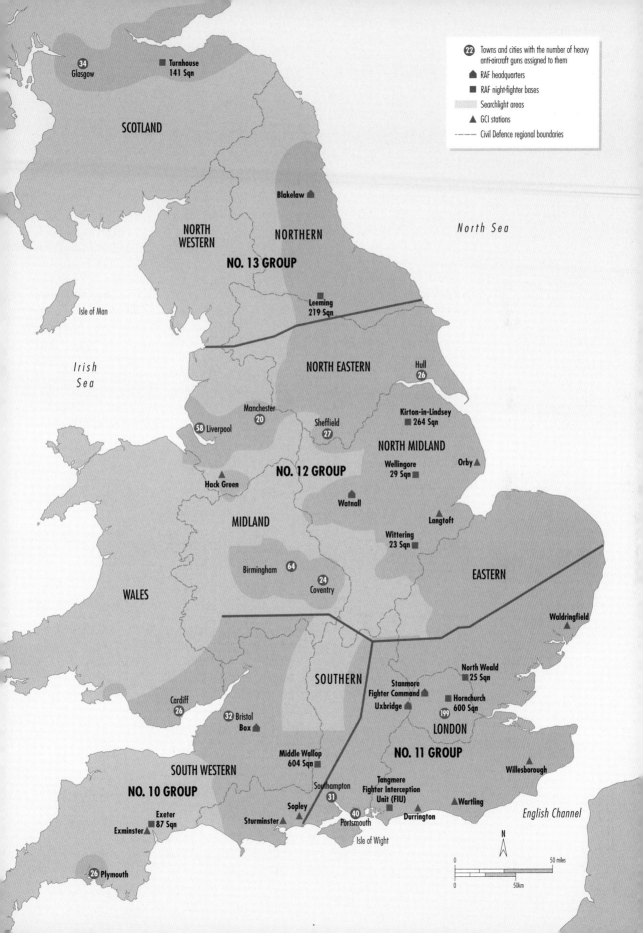

	Towns and cities with the number of heavy anti-aircraft guns assigned to them
22	Towns and cities with the number of heavy anti-aircraft guns assigned to them
⬟	RAF headquarters
■	RAF night-fighter bases
▨	Searchlight areas
▲	GCI stations
– – –	Civil Defence regional boundaries

SCOTLAND

34 Glasgow

■ Turnhouse
141 Sqn

North Sea

NORTH WESTERN

NORTHERN

NO. 13 GROUP

Blakelaw ⬟

Isle of Man

Irish Sea

Leeming
219 Sqn

NORTH EASTERN

Hull
26

Manchester
20

Sheffield
27

Kirton-in-Lindsey
■ 264 Sqn

58 Liverpool

NORTH MIDLAND

Wellingore
29 Sqn ■

Orby ▲

NO. 12 GROUP

Hack Green ▲

Watnall ⬟

Langtoft ▲

MIDLAND

Wittering
23 Sqn ■

EASTERN

WALES

Birmingham
64

Coventry
24

Waldringfield ▲

Cardiff
26

32 Bristol
Box ⬟

North Weald
■ 25 Sqn

Stanmore
Fighter Command ⬟
Uxbridge ⬟

Hornchurch
■ 600 Sqn

199

LONDON

SOUTHERN

NO. 11 GROUP

Middle Wallop
604 Sqn ■

Willesborough ▲

SOUTH WESTERN

Southampton

Tangmere
Fighter Interception
Unit (FIU) ■

Wartling ▲

NO. 10 GROUP

Sopley ▲

31

40

Durrington ▲

English Channel

Exeter
■ 87 Sqn

Exminster ▲

Sturminster ▲

Portsmouth

Isle of Wight

N

26 Plymouth

0   50 miles

0   50km

By 1938, the government realised that there were not enough shelters for all. A partial solution was the humble corrugated steel Anderson shelter, which could be dug into a back yard or garden. The Anderson proved remarkably resilient: here, many have survived in a London neighbourhood largely flattened by bombing. (Fox Photos/ Stringer, Getty)

leadership of Wg Cdr Edward Addison, was up and running. Dr Robert Cockburn of the Telecommunications Research Establishment headed the small team that hand-built the jamming transmitters. Initially, these were modified hospital diathermy sets, which with a jamming power of only 150 watts, were of doubtful practical value.

A purpose-built remedy for the 'Headache' posed by *Knickebein*, known (with tongue-in-cheek humour) as 'Aspirin', was soon ready. Aspirin radiated unsynchronized Morse dashes on the German frequencies at a power of 500 watts. These dashes were 'superimposed' over the German signals. Thus, when a bomber entered the 'dash zone' and turned to find the 'steady note zone', the aircraft's radio operator continued to hear dashes. When the bomber continued to move into the 'dot zone', the operator heard dots and dashes and confusion would follow.

Post-war legend has it that 80 Wing 'bent the beams' and *Knickebein* fell into disuse from an early stage as a consequence. Research by the late Dr Alfred Price revealed that this was not the case. Surviving Luftwaffe crews stated that the genuine *Knickebein* signals could be detected through 80 Wing's jamming. Aspirin did prove to the Luftwaffe that the RAF was aware of *Knickebein*. This fact provoked the anxiety that night fighters could be used to 'hunt in the beam' for German bombers. In consequence, there was a reluctance by crews to use the *Knickebein* beam over Britain and, from early in the Blitz, recourse was made to navigation visually by moonlight. In fact, night-fighter patrols inside the *Knickebein* beam were tried by Fighter Command, without success.

'Meacons'

The Air Intelligence Branch and 80 Wing quickly devised a way of interfering with the Luftwaffe's radio beacon network in France and Belgium. An RAF radio station received the German beacon signals and relayed them to a nearby transmitter, or Masking Beacon ('Meacon'). If the location of the Meacon was in a geographical location which approximately mimicked the position of a real Luftwaffe radio beacon (for example, near a coastline or an estuary), it was possible to confuse tired and lost Luftwaffe crews. By August, there were 15 Meacon stations in Britain and their effectiveness (admittedly difficult to quantify) increased as more stations were added. A variety of other countermeasures, such as decoy sites (which led to the 'Starfish' programme), the Long Aerial Mine, the Free Balloon Barrage and Intruder patrols, were tried as the Blitz went on.

Aspirin and Meacon were at least partially successful and both were in operation before the Blitz began in earnest. The more sophisticated bombing aids, *X*- and *Y-Gerät*, were not discovered until the campaign was underway. The decision to use (and thus reveal) *Knickebein* before the opening of the night offensive has been construed as a mistake, although it must be remembered that the Luftwaffe still did not envisage a large-scale night offensive over Britain in the summer of 1940.

Guns and searchlights

In the absence of an effective night-fighter force, it was Anti-Aircraft (AA) Command which shouldered the burden of defence. Although an army formation, commanded from October 1939, by Lt Gen Sir Frederick Pile, operational control was exercised by Fighter Command. In 1940–41, the great majority of AA Command's personnel were drawn from the Territorial Army.

The Command's most numerous weapon was the 3.7in. gun. This fired a shell with a ceiling of around 25,000ft at a maximum rate of about ten rounds per minute. The shells were time-fused and on explosion produced a burst of steel splinters with a lethal radius of some 45ft. In addition, a newer 4.5in. gun had begun to enter service. In September 1939, the 'approved scale' of heavy AA guns was 2,232 but by July 1940 there were still only some 1,200 heavy AA guns of all types in UK service, not all of which were the modern 3.7in. or 4.5in. types.

There were usually four, six or eight guns to a battery. Each battery was equipped with a height-finder and a predictor. The height-finder sent information to the predictor which then worked out the target's flightpath. The necessary 'firing solution' could be calculated: the *azimuth* (bearing) and elevation (height) settings for the gun and the time fusing for the shell. Even in clear visibility, an aircraft that changed course, height, speed, or a combination of these, made accurate prediction difficult to the point of impossibility. If there was no information for the guns, they resorted to firing 'barrages' over certain geographical points, either based on the likely location of any enemy aircraft within range, or on a line ahead of which the attackers were predicted to drop their bombs.

Sir Frederick Pile (left) headed AA Command from the first day of the war to the last. AA Command's guns may have brought down few raiders but the London Barrage (described by more than one witness as a 'roar') helped to keep up spirits. (Bill Brandt/Stringer, Getty)

Working with the guns was a network of searchlights. In the summer of 1940, the most common searchlight was the 36in. (90cm) type of 210 million candlepower. During the

Female sound locator operators, wearing their service respirators, during an exercise in May 1940. AA Command was still awaiting deliveries of an effective gun-laying radar. Early experience in September 1940 proved the manifest shortcomings of sound location. (Central press/Stringer, Getty)

Blitz, the 60in. (150cm), 510 million candlepower, searchlight began to be issued. Clouds, moonlight and the height of the attacking aircraft all affected searchlight effectiveness. Even when later guided by radar, the searchlights were not especially successful and rarely assisted in destroying enemy aircraft. In September 1939, AA Command deployed 2,700 searchlights out of an approved total of 4,128.

At the outbreak of war and in the first months of the Blitz, AA Command relied on sound locators when cloud or darkness concealed enemy aircraft. In theory, the locators would provide the searchlights with the approximate location of the aircraft. When the target was found and 'coned' by the searchlights, the guns would engage. It was quickly realized that the problems inherent with this equipment were insurmountable. The standard sound locator had a maximum range of three and a half miles, from which it took 18 seconds for the sound of the aircraft to reach the locator. More time was needed to work out the predicted flightpath of the target, aim the guns and fuse the shell. By then, almost a minute would have elapsed and the aircraft, which could only be approximately located in any case, would have travelled four to six miles. If there were several bombers in the vicinity, their engine noise 'swamped' the locators, rendering them useless.

The first Gun Laying Mk I radar (GL Mk I) entered service in 1939 and there were some 300 by summer 1940. The set could identify an aircraft's range accurately but azimuth measurement was imprecise and elevation could not be calculated at all. GL Mk I was of limited use and a successor, GL Mk II, offered improvement in azimuth accuracy and an ability to calculate elevation. This device was undergoing trials by the summer of 1940 but suffered numerous teething troubles. Entry into service was delayed until October, when a small number became available to the guns defending London.

Barrage balloons

The final link in the ground defences was the low zone barrage balloon. A balloon barrage flew at a maximum height of 5,000ft and was intended to force attacking aircraft to fly at higher altitudes. This diminished bombing accuracy while simultaneously allowing the aircraft to be engaged by the heavy guns in the area. The barrage balloon became one of the most recognizable symbols of the British Home Front in general and the Blitz in particular.

Low zone barrage balloons, or 'Pigs'. Concentrated around target key points, the balloons proved very effective in keeping enemy aircraft at altitude, drastically reducing bombing accuracy. Like the searchlight, the barrage balloon quickly became inextricably linked to the 'Home Front'. (IWM CH 1522 (AHB))

If a German bomber was unfortunate enough to hit a balloon cable, the sudden shock of impact caused cutting links to sever each end of the cable, from which small parachutes would deploy. The opened parachutes generated drag equal to approximately six times the thrust of the aircraft's engines. This was enough to bring the bomber to a violent halt, at which point it stalled and fell out of the sky. As the cable was pulled by the aircraft, a wire ripped away a portion of the balloon's fabric, causing it to drop gently to the ground.

The balloons only accounted for, at most, 30 enemy aircraft during the entire war. Despite this unpromising figure, there is no record of any low-flying German bomber or dive-bomber making a deliberate attack on a target protected by a balloon barrage. In July 1940, when a new requirement of 2,600 balloons was estimated, there were 1,466 balloons available out of a nominal establishment of 1,865.

The 'Magic Mirrors': airborne interception radar
Interception, whether by day or night, needed to satisfy three problems:

1. A method of detecting enemy aircraft approaching Britain with accuracy and in good time.
2. An efficient method of directing the interceptors to the enemy aircraft.
3. Interceptors with the performance and firepower to engage and destroy the enemy aircraft.

By the outbreak of war, the Chain Home (CH) radar stations and the associated method of reporting, tracking and interception provided a good defence against the daylight raider. There was, however, no real solution to finding and destroying hostile aircraft in poor weather or at night. The night-time defensive tactics of the 1930s were little changed from those employed during World War I. Enemy bombers were expected to make their attacks in moonlit conditions, when they could be illuminated by searchlight crews and engaged by anti-aircraft guns and single-seat fighters. In the 1934 Air Exercises, only two out of five bombers were intercepted – despite flying with their navigation lights on.

In 1936, the radar pioneer Robert Watson-Watt proposed that the solution lay with a miniaturized radar carried by an interceptor. After early trials proved the idea's feasibility,

A Bristol Blenheim Mk IF of 25 Sqn taxying at Martlesham Heath, 25 July 1940. These aircraft were equipped with AI Mk III radar. However, experience showed that the radar was unreliable and difficult to use. The Blenheim's lacklustre performance meant that occasional fleeting 'contacts' were almost invariably lost. (IWM HU 104653)

gradual improvements were made in range and accuracy. Experience with Airborne Interception (AI) Mk I and Mk II radar (nicknamed 'Magic Mirrors') between May 1939 and the summer of 1940 confirmed that another challenge was to make a device reliable enough for service conditions.

The first set to see widespread service use was AI Mk III. The maximum range was 17,000ft but minimum range was poor: the operator's cathode ray tube often 'lost' the target before it could be seen by the pilot. In addition, the target's bearing could become confused, frustrating any chance of visual contact being made. This last problem was partially solved by modification of the set to AI Mk IIIA standard. The new equipment proved astonishingly unreliable. Only 10 per cent of cathode ray tubes supplied were usable and surviving aircrew reports are peppered with references to severe shocks from the gun button and interceptions being abandoned when the radar sets began to burn. Some of the interception techniques tried between late 1939 and September 1940 included:

- AI fighters flying on fixed patrol lines, usually at points where enemy aircraft were expected to cross the coast, or on routes to a target. Radar contacts were rare, visual contacts rarer still and successful combats almost unknown.
- Attempted interceptions by AI fighters out to sea, using information provided by the CH radar network. CH was only able to 'look' out to sea and determine the location of aircraft with an accuracy of three to five miles, which did not permit successful interceptions.
- Attempted interceptions by AI fighters over land, using information provided by the Observer Corps. The information from the Observer Corps was vague and invariably out of date by the time it was relayed to the fighter's crew.

Whatever the method used, the same problems persisted: the difficulty of guiding the fighter to an interception, coupled with the lethargic performance of the AI-equipped fighter: the Blenheim Mk IF. The results say everything: in June, July and August, just 22 German aircraft were 'claimed' at night, from an estimated total of 6,944 Luftwaffe sorties.

Help was at hand, for on 30 June 1940 trials began with AI Mk IV. The new set featured improved minimum and maximum ranges and was earmarked for the new Bristol Beaufighter Mk IF. Work was also proceeding on the Ground Controlled Interception (GCI) system, which employed a ground-based rotating radar aerial, giving the operator a 360° view. Although a medium range radar, it promised to revolutionize night-fighter guidance – when it entered service.

The hastily designed Beaufighter suffered extended teething problems on entry into service. The aircraft went on to become one of World War II's great night fighters, when paired with Ground Controlled Interception radar. These are 600 Sqn night fighters based at Colerne in 1941. (IWM CH 17265 (AHB))

The aircraft

The Blenheim was descended from the Bristol Type 142, a fast business aircraft built for the newspaper magnate Lord Rothermere and named 'Britain First'. This first flew in 1935 and displayed a startling turn of speed. Impressed, the Air Ministry drew Specification B.28/35 around Bristol's proposed new light bomber version, the Type 142M. By September 1935, a batch of 150 aircraft had been ordered and the Blenheim Mk I entered service in March 1937. The Blenheim was an advanced all-metal monoplane with an enclosed cockpit, retractable undercarriage and a powered dorsal gun turret. Although regarded as a formidable light bomber on entry into service, the Blenheim was already outdated by 1940.

From 1938, a long-range fighter variant, the Mk IF, began to enter service, armed with a ventral four-gun pack. In July 1939, the aircraft became the world's first radar-equipped night fighter when it was selected for AI conversion. AI-equipped Blenheims were initially distributed in ones and twos in 25, 29, 141, 600 (which formed the nucleus of the Fighter

The Boulton Paul Defiant proved a failure with 141 and 264 Sqns in the Battle of Britain. By contrast, the aircraft would go on to have a very successful career as a night fighter. This 264 Sqn Defiant Mk I was based at West Malling during the latter stages of the campaign. (IWM CH 3448 (AHB))

Interception Unit: FIU), 601 and 604 Sqns. The Blenheims enjoyed very little success before or during the subsequent campaign. They were too slow to intercept the German bombers with any certainty and their armament was insufficient to cripple a German bomber on the rare occasions when contact was made. A typical entry in 29 Squadron's Operations Record Book (ORB) reads:

23 September 1940. Time: 00.40: Blenheim ordered up to investigate hostile raid. The searchlights were good and two interceptions were made, but both bandits were flying

A Douglas Havoc Mk I (Intruder) of 23 Sqn, based at Ford in Sussex, 1941. The Havoc was well-liked by crews, especially after their experience with the Blenheim. The Intruder variant of the Havoc was not equipped with AI radar, in case it fell into enemy hands over Europe. (IWM CH 2786 (AHB))

in the opposite direction to and above the Blenheim. By the time the pilot had turned the Blenheim both bandits were out of sight and not seen again. The AI went out of order.

The Bristol Beaufighter was conceived in the days following the 1938 Munich Agreement, when the Air Ministry realized a long-range heavy fighter was needed to replace the stop-gap Blenheim Mk IF. Bristol responded by using the flying surfaces and undercarriage of the Beaufort torpedo bomber (itself a descendant of the Blenheim), together with the Hercules engine, to rapidly produce the Type 156 Beaufighter. The prototype flew in July 1939 and the Air Ministry had already ordered large contracts before the first examples were accepted by the RAF.

The Beaufighter's roomy fuselage lent itself to the installation of AI radar and the aircraft was envisaged as a night fighter from an early stage. A heavy armament of four Hispano cannons and six machine guns was specified, although the first 50 examples were armed only with cannons. The AI operator (known as the observer and later as the radio navigator) had his own Perspex 'bubble' behind the pilot. One of the operator's more unenviable duties was reloading the early drum-fed 20mm cannons.

Although the Beaufighter entered service only relatively slowly, due to a host of teething problems, the new aircraft proved itself to be everything the Blenheim was not. The 29 Sqn ORB for 18 September 1940 was enthusiastic:

The machine appears a very popular aircraft with those who have flown it. Although no speed test [was] made, it appears easily able to hold a Hurricane. It is not much more difficult to fly at night than a Blenheim… the machine generally is more pleasant at night than a Blenheim owing to its superior manoeuvrability.

Another aircraft which saw much action as a night fighter during the Blitz was the Boulton Paul Defiant. Originally designed as a day interceptor equipped with a four-gun-powered turret, the Defiant famously possessed no fixed forward-firing armament – although the turret could be turned to fire forwards.

The aircraft proved a failure in its intended role, suffering heavy losses in combat with the Messerschmitt Bf109. The two Defiant squadrons were withdrawn from the daylight battle and reassigned to 'cat's eye' night-fighter duties on the very eve of the Blitz. By May 1941, the Defiant wholly or partially equipped seven squadrons. The aircraft was outstandingly successful in the night-fighter role and claimed more enemy aircraft than any of its contemporaries over the course of the Blitz. On 15 March 1941, the 96 Sqn ORB glowingly recorded that, 'Pilots are coming to recognise that the Defiant is the best single-engined night fighter.'

The Hawker Hurricane and Supermarine Spitfire were used as 'cat's eyes' fighters before and during the Blitz. Dowding was reluctant to authorize their use on any but the brightest of moonlit nights, fearing, not without justification, that their accident rate would be prohibitively high. Night flying was notoriously unsafe for the pilots of single-seat fighters. The narrow-track undercarriage of the Spitfire made it especially unsuitable for night landings but the Hurricane, after various modifications, would see considerable service as a night fighter after Dowding's retirement. In addition, the Hurricanes of 87 Sqn began operations in the Intruder role from March 1941.

After the fall of France, 147 Douglas DB-7 light bombers were diverted to the UK. The aircraft was renamed the Havoc and modified into two different night-fighter versions. The Mk I was fitted with eight Browning machine guns, AI Mk IV radar and entered service with 85 Sqn in February 1941. The Havoc Mk I (Intruder) entered service with 23 Sqn a month later. This variant was not equipped with AI, for fears that it could be captured if an aircraft came down over Europe. The Havocs were large but fast, powerful and rugged, and came to be well-liked by their crews.

Type	Max speed	Ceiling	Armament
Bristol Blenheim Mk IF	260mph	27,280ft	5 x 0.303 machine guns
Bristol Beaufighter Mk IF	323mph	28,900ft	4 x 20mm cannon and 6 x 0.303 machine guns
Boulton Paul Defiant Mk I	304mph	30,350ft	4 x 0.303 machine guns
Douglas Havoc Mk I	295mph	25,800ft	8 x 0.303 machine guns
Douglas Havoc Mk I (Intruder)	295mph	25,800ft	4 x 0.303 machine guns 2,400lb of bombs

Commanders

The Commander-in-Chief of RAF Fighter Command when the Blitz began was the austere but perceptive figure of Sir Hugh Dowding. His interest in new technology was in evidence from an early age. Dowding learned to fly in 1913, joined the Royal Flying Corps in 1914 and in 1915 was put in command of a squadron. He remained in the RAF at the end of World War I and his efficient style of leadership was recognized by a series of promotions. In 1929, he was made Air Officer Commanding Fighting Area, Air Defence of Great Britain (essentially the forerunner to 11 Group Fighter Command). Dowding's technical knowledge ensured he joined the Air Council as Air Member for Supply and Research in 1935, where he played a key role in the development of CH and AI radar.

Air Chief Marshal Sir Hugh Dowding led Fighter Command as the Battle of Britain gave way to the Blitz. He had supported the airborne radar experiments of the late 1930s but his perceived intransigence in matters of day and night air defence led to his 'retirement' in November 1941. (Mirrorpix/Contributor, Getty)

Dowding was the outstanding choice to lead Fighter Command and in the battles of France and Britain he more than repaid the trust vested in him. Known as 'Stuffy' for his quiet demeanour, Dowding was nevertheless a clear-thinking and progressive officer. His retirement was deferred several times and on 25 November 1940, as the Blitz was entering a new phase, he was replaced by one of his leading critics, Sir William Sholto Douglas.

As Deputy Chief of the Air Staff, Sholto Douglas had sided with those who argued for a more aggressive defence, employing the 'Big Wing' in daylight and single-seat fighters by night. The appointment of Sir Charles Portal as Chief of the Air Staff in October 1940 cleared the way for a number of changes at senior level and Sholto Douglas was one of the beneficiaries. He immediately pressed for more night-fighter squadrons and the GCI system to be introduced as quickly as possible. Fighter Command would be led by Sholto Douglas for the remainder of the Blitz.

CAMPAIGN OBJECTIVES
Bringing Britain to its knees

September 1940 and from left to right, Luftwaffe Chief of Staff Hans Jeschonnek, commander of II Fliegerkorps General Bruno Lörzer, Göring and adjutant Bernd von Brauchitsch consider their options. The decision to attack London is often viewed as a mistake but by early September Hitler may have already decided to postpone *Seelöwe*. (ullstein bild Dtl./Contributor, Getty)

The war aim of the British, as in the last war, is to bring Germany to her knees by severing our entire foreign trade… Britain may most effectively be weakened by attacks on her overseas trade… Germany must therefore as a counter-measure attempt to sever the Motherland from her overseas sources of supply.

Oberst Joseph Schmid, 22 November 1939

For Germany, the answer to the dilemma presented by a future conflict with Britain lay with the traditional strategy of *Handelskrieg* (trade war), as a way of 'counter-blockading the blockader'. This time, Germany would not have to rely solely on U-boats and commerce raiders: advances in navigation and bomb-carrying capacity meant the Luftwaffe could now play a part by attacking British ships and ports.

In 1939, the Luftwaffe produced two studies dealing with the best way to approach a campaign against Britain. Perhaps tellingly, each came to a different conclusion. The first, a report made after air exercises by Luftflotte 2 in May 1939, found inadequacies in the number of available bombers and in bomber crew training. 'Terror attacks' on the civilian population (previously dismissed in any case in LDv 16) were seen as ineffectual at best and counter-productive at worst.

The second – and more important – was *Studie Blau*, published by Schmid's 5th Abteilung in June 1939. This 94-page report was the fruit of several months of work by experts in industry, economics, foreign trade, technology and politics. The result, described by Göring as 'comprehensive', was in fact a hastily written document which made some superficial and arbitrary conclusions. *Studie Blau* played down the ability of the RAF to defend the British Isles, while overemphasizing the Luftwaffe's own striking power. Ports and shipping were considered vital to the British war effort and to be especially vulnerable to air attack. For all its inadequacies and undue confidence, *Studie Blau* was in some respects a diligent piece of

Air Marshal Sir William Sholto Douglas. Although energetic in leadership, there was little Sholto Douglas could do until technical improvements in the AI and GCI equipment came on stream in the spring of 1941. (Fox Photos/Stringer, Getty)

work and became the foundation for the Luftwaffe's future operations against Britain. Yet by mid-1940, much of the information on which it was based was out of date.

Führer Directive No 1 defined the 'dislocation of English imports' as a Luftwaffe objective as early as 31 August 1939. Three months later, Hitler issued Führer Directive No 9:

The defeat of England is essential to final victory. The most effective means of ensuring this is to cripple the English economy by attacking it at decisive points... The Navy and Air Force will then carry out the following tasks, given in the order of importance:

a. Attacks on the principal English ports by mining and blocking the sea lanes leading to them, and by the destruction of important port installations...

b. Attacks on English merchant shipping...

c. Destruction of English depots, oil storage plants, food in cold storage, and grain stores...

e. The destruction of industrial plants ... in particular key points of the aircraft industry...

This policy of economic blockade was overtaken by events when France surrendered in June 1940. This sudden and unexpected victory left Hitler three options with regard to Britain.

The first was to make peace with the British government. On 19 July, Hitler made 'a final appeal to reason' to Britain. The rejection of his 'offer' left Hitler with the choice of either continuing the policy of the counter-blockade or mounting a seaborne invasion of Britain. The first entailed a long-term commitment – indeed, on 23 May, Hitler confided that he doubted Britain could be defeated by air power alone and that to do so would

Britain's decision to fight on after the fall of France left Hitler with a strategic dilemma. This was soon complicated by his ally, Italian dictator Benito Mussolini, whose campaigns in the Balkans and Mediterranean quickly went awry. Hitler, meanwhile, was increasingly preoccupied with the Soviet Union. (Mark Wilson/Staff, Getty)

require a long campaign involving all available resources. An invasion offered the possibility of knocking Britain out of the war quickly, leaving Germany free to concentrate on the Soviet Union.

Ultimately, Hitler chose to pursue both options. The Kriegsmarine and Luftwaffe would continue to target British merchant and naval shipping, while planning began for an invasion of southern England, codenamed Operation *Seelöwe* (Sealion). On 6 August, Kesselring, Sperrle and Stumpff (the commander of Luftflotte 5, based in Norway) were summoned to Carinhall, Göring's luxurious country house, for a final meeting before *Adlertag* (Eagle Day). Basing their planning on Schmid's optimistic assessments and assumptions, their objectives were:

1. The neutralization of Fighter Command through aerial combat and bombing airfields, to attain air superiority over southern England. Attacks would then move to:
2. Destruction of Bomber and Coastal Command units that could interfere with a cross-Channel operation.
3. Destruction of naval units in ports and at sea along the English southern coast, but only if 'particularly favourable' targets presented themselves.
4. Harassing (night) attacks against ports, communications, aircraft and aero-engine factories, RAF depots and bomber airfields.

Accordingly, from 12 August, the Luftwaffe began a series of heavy attacks against radar stations and airfields in southern England. Between 12 August and 6 September, the critical phase of the Battle of Britain, 53 major attacks were made on British airfields, only 32 of which were Fighter Command bases. Just six major strikes were made against radar sites but over 1,000 raids of all sizes were made on a variety of minor targets. Overall, the Luftwaffe's campaign lacked focus and did not come close to delivering the knockout blow envisaged by its commanders. The fighting in the air was scarcely more successful for the Luftwaffe. Both sides suffered heavy aircrew losses. Combat fatigue, christened '*Kanalkrankheit*' ('Channel sickness') by the Luftwaffe, became increasingly common as the fighting went on.

On 19 August, Göring met his commanders again at Carinhall. Armed with another set of Schmid's figures, Göring ordered the second phase of the campaign to begin. While Luftflotte 2 flew heavily escorted raids to draw up the remaining RAF fighters, Luftflotte 3 would concentrate on a night-bombing campaign against RAF Bomber Command bases, ports and industrial towns.

Between 1 July and 11 August 1940, German bombers flew an estimated 575 nocturnal sorties against the UK. Between 12 and 25 August, this number increased to 925. In all, the Luftwaffe made over 3,000 sorties in darkness on the UK before 7 September. While material damage was slight, the raids disrupted production by causing air raid alerts on an almost nightly basis. Furthermore, the flights provided night-flying practice for the Luftwaffe aircrews. The 'Blitz proper' is often seen as beginning on 7 September, yet in August alone, 1,149 civilians were killed by bombing, with another 1,530 injured. For these victims, as well as the thousands left bereaved or homeless, the German night-bombing campaign was already a brutal reality.

'WANTED for incitement to MURDER. This gangster, who you see in his element...', fulminated German propaganda. Winston Churchill holds an American-made Thompson sub-machine gun in July 1940. The rejection of Hitler's peace offer by Churchill's government that same month left German strategists with the question: What now? (IWM/Getty Images/Contributor)

A Heinkel He 111 of KG 1 lies on its belly in a field, 30 August 1940. As August turned to September, heavy losses caused by seemingly undiminished numbers of British fighters prompted the Luftflotten commanders to look at other ways of defeating Fighter Command. (A.J. O'Brien/ Stringer, Getty)

As part of this move towards the bombing of economic and military targets, Luftflotte 3 made four consecutive night attacks on Liverpool and Birkenhead between 28 and 31 August. Although important, the port (codenamed *Speisekammer*: 'Pantry') had no direct influence on the Battle of Britain and the raids were seemingly a 'dress rehearsal' for the German crews. The attacks themselves were ineffective. Those on the first and second nights were marred by bombing inaccuracy. The third raid inflicted some damage to suburban property. It was the fourth night when Liverpool suffered. Some 160 fires were reported in the city centre but the docks were only lightly damaged. Many other towns and cities were struck on these nights by bombers operating in small numbers across Britain.

It was in this period, between the last week of August and the first week of September, when the Battle of Britain merged with the Blitz. On 3 September, with time running short before a final decision on *Seelöwe* could be made, Göring and his commanders held a conference in The Hague. Schmid had prepared yet another calculation of Fighter Command's strength. Although he had revised the figures once more, they were still unduly optimistic. Meanwhile, German losses for August were 774 from all causes, or 18.5 per cent of all combat aircraft available at the beginning of the month. The daylight campaign was becoming unsustainable.

Confusion and disagreement over strategy developed between the two Luftflotten. Sperrle argued for continued attacks on Fighter Command's infrastructure. Kesselring, whose Luftflotte 2 had taken the heaviest losses, had been investigating for some days the possibility of drawing out Fighter Command with a large-scale strike against London. Others, such as *Oberkommando der Wehrmacht* (OKW: Wehrmacht High Command) Chief of Operations General Alfred Jodl, had been arguing for such attacks since June. In Jodl's view, the inevitable civilian casualties and depletion of food stocks would break morale in the capital and force Churchill's government to surrender. Despite a complete lack of evidence, Göring, Chief of Staff Hans Jeschonnek and the Foreign Ministry's 'England Committee' agreed: bombing London might cause mass panic and political upheaval.

These men were pushing against an open door. On the night of 24/25 August, a Heinkel He 111, attempting to find the Rochester and Thames Haven oil refineries in the darkness, accidentally dropped its payload over the boroughs of East Ham and Bethnal Green.

Churchill interpreted this as an escalation of the air war into indiscriminate bombing of civilian-populated areas and ordered retaliatory attacks on Berlin. Bomber Command duly raided Berlin on 25/26 and 28/29 August, inflicting minor damage. On 30 August, an incensed Hitler lifted his ban on bombing London. Five days later, in words notable for their remarkably unhappy irony, the Führer told a mainly female audience at the Berlin *Sportpalast*: 'When they [the British] declare that they will increase their attacks on our cities, then we will raze their cities to the ground. The hour will come when one of us will break, and it will not be National Socialist Germany.'

The aims of the Blitz at its outset were therefore a mix of political, economic and military objectives. In summary, these were:

1. To force Dowding's fighters to accept battle with Kesselring's Messerschmitt Bf 109 *Jagdgruppen*. In this 'target rich' environment, the remaining Spitfires and Hurricanes would be destroyed, paving the way for Operation *Seelöwe*.
2. To 'strike at the heart' of the enemy. This somewhat ill-defined objective meant, in reality, attacking the Port of London, in line with the traditional emphasis on attacks on Britain's economy. As such, it was the beginning of a long-term strategy – which may have been Hitler's intention.
3. To cause a catastrophic loss of morale. The effect of the air attacks could, it was reasoned, produce widespread social and political discontent, perhaps forcing the British government to capitulate and rendering an invasion unnecessary. The timeframe needed for this was uncertain.
4. To sate the German population's supposed desire for revenge for the bombing of Berlin and to deter further Bomber Command attacks. This was the politically motivated aim alluded to by Hitler in his *Sportpalast* speech.

The Luftwaffe was thus committed to a campaign on London, for an uncertain length of time and with a variety of different objectives. Although this moment marked the opening of what many see as the 'Blitz proper', the Luftwaffe's aims would continue to evolve in the ensuing weeks and months of the campaign.

THE CAMPAIGN
The enemy strikes

I personally have assumed leadership of this attack … in which for the first time the German Luftwaffe has struck at the heart of the enemy.

Reichsmarschall Hermann Göring, radio broadcast, 7 September 1940

'Loge' (London Gebiet: London area): The London campaign, 7 September–13 November

The Blitz begins, 7 September–13 October

Saturday, 7 September 1940, the day on which Göring inaugurated the campaign against London, would forever after be known in the capital as 'Black Saturday'. A daylight raid by 348 bombers from five Kampfgeschwader left hundreds of fires in the dock area between North Woolwich and Tower Bridge. They were still burning when 318 bombers from Luftflotte 3 returned that evening. The power stations at Battersea and West Ham were hit and forced to shut down. At the Surrey Commercial Docks, where soft woods and grain from the Baltic and North America were imported, a thousand fire pumps fought the flames. Around 80 per cent of the 1½ million tons of wood stored there was destroyed by fire. Asphyxiating paint and rubber fires raged unchecked, while burning pepper scorched the lungs of those nearby. Molten grain produced a treacle-like substance, which adhered to the boots of the firemen. At the West India Docks, millions of litres of rum flowed in burning torrents into the river. Intense heat blistered the paint on fireboats and caused quayside cranes to buckle and crash into the water. Thames barges, their tethers burned through, drifted down the current, only to return hours later on the incoming tide. The unexpected attacks killed 436 people and seriously injured another 1,600.

Late afternoon, 7 September 1940: London's long ordeal has begun. This He 111 is directly over the Upper Pool of London. The Western Dock and a portion of the St Katharine Docks can be seen in front of the port wing. The hard-hit Surrey Commercial Docks are visible behind the starboard wing. (IWM C 5422 (AHB))

This was just the beginning. The Luftwaffe tried daylight attacks on London again, notably on 11 and 15 September, and suffered further losses. Two days later, with air superiority clearly out of reach, Hitler postponed *Seelöwe,* but Göring, armed with Schmid's inaccurate estimates of Fighter Command strength, continued to dispatch further large daylight raids. The last came on 30 September, when 46 German aircraft failed to return. In the ensuing weeks, Messerschmitt Bf 109 fighter-bombers made high-altitude attacks on London, in unsuccessful attempts to goad Dowding's fighters into combat. Despite these efforts, the daylight battle phase gradually petered out.

The night assault

One German airman compared the uneventful monotony of the Luftwaffe's nights over London in September 1940 to running a bus service. The night offensive, quickly nicknamed the 'Blitz' by the British press, continued to target London's dock areas, railway communications and power stations. Lying at the heart of a glittering web of railway lines, London was easy to find and the serpentine bend of the Thames clearly marked the centre. The Luftwaffe codename for the London dock area, *Seéschlange* ('Sea snake'), was no coincidence. Moreover, the capital, just 90 miles from the French coast, was only half an hour's flying time away. Weather permitting, some crews could fly twice or even three times to London in one night. The *Krokodil* of bombers which flew steadily in single file to and from London night after night added to the strain for the population by keeping the city under alert as long as possible – often between eight and ten hours.

The maps issued to aircrews marked zones and even specific targets in precise rhomboids and circles. Yet while London was impossible to miss, a host of factors combined to reduce the campaign's effectiveness. Surviving German airmen recalled that the little night-flying training they received had not prepared them for the Blitz, which imposed a different kind of strain to that of the daylight battles. *Knickebein* was not sufficiently accurate for precision bombing. The *X-Gerät*-equipped KGr 100 He 111s were gradually withdrawn from precision attacks and instead employed as pathfinders, marking, for example, Piccadilly Circus on 17/18 September and the Handley Page factory at Cricklewood five days later. Target-marking methods were rudimentary. Frequent spells of poor weather

An anonymous Junkers Ju 88, wearing black 'Blitz' camouflage on its under surfaces, awaits the coming night's operations. This image was taken in October 1940, as the Luftwaffe inaugurated *Mondscheinserenade Loge* against the British capital. (Keystone-France/ Contributor, Getty)

in late September did nothing to improve the bombers' accident rate, or target location and bombing accuracy. Together, these did more to blunt the night campaign than the defences.

The bombing certainly seemed indiscriminate to London's inhabitants. The southern and eastern parts of London remained the most heavily hit but there were scenes of destruction all over the city. The bombing during the early weeks of the Blitz caused damage to many famous buildings, including the City Guildhall, the Tower of London, Buckingham Palace, 145 Piccadilly (the former home of the then Princess Elizabeth), various hospitals including St Thomas', the Houses of Parliament and St Paul's Cathedral. The heaviest raid of the period came on 18/19 September, when 300 aircraft dropped 350 tons of high explosive bombs and 628 containers of incendiaries.

The conflict over future strategy

Following the postponement of *Seelöwe* on 17 September, Hitler began to turn his interest elsewhere. Left with an independent air offensive he neither expected nor wanted, Göring likewise showed little further interest. After this point, the precise aim of the Luftwaffe becomes less clear. There was little consensus within OKL, Schmid's own intelligence section or the Foreign Ministry's England Committee.

The focus, at least nominally, remained on the British economy. Major raids continued on the London dock area with minor attacks on ports and industrial towns. While Hitler forbade 'terror attacks', civilian morale was clearly a target, no matter the claims to the contrary. Goebbels confided in his diary on 12 September that great care was needed to maintain the appearance of attacks against military targets.

On the same day, a Luftwaffe intelligence study, 'Assessment of the Situation of Great Britain', suggested attacks continue on London's docks and utilities. Attacking other parts of the capital would be useful only if industrial areas – and workers' residential districts – were bombed. The same paper also proposed major attacks on the aircraft and armaments industries of the Midlands. On 14 September, an OKW directive also ordered that attacks concentrate on targets vital to the war effort and the essential functioning of the city. Six days later, the England Committee suggested that there was no need to refrain from attacking the civilian population. It added, rather hopefully, that attacks on working class districts would cause workers to move to west London, causing a breach between the classes.

On the same day as the England Committee submitted its memorandum, a note from the Intelligence Staff recommended that the focus should remain on the London docks and the electricity, gas and water utilities in London. This, it argued, would not only impair the port but affect public health. Even if attacks were restricted to limited target areas, the effects would be felt by the civilian population through scattered bombing and emergency bomb jettisoning. The note also suggested that attacks should be made on the industries of the Midlands, including Birmingham, Sheffield and Coventry.

Disagreements over attacks against the population had in reality become academic. An official 'guess' by the British government suggested that in the first six weeks of the London Blitz, 16,000 houses were destroyed or damaged beyond repair, 60,000 were seriously damaged but repairable and 130,000 were slightly damaged.

The London Blitz renewed

On 7 October, Göring announced a 'new plan' in Berlin. He then went on leave until 1941. The directive demanded:

1. Absolute control of the Channel and the English coastal areas.
2. Progressive and complete annihilation of London, with all its military objectives and industrial production.
3. A steady paralysing of Britain's technical, commercial, industrial and civil life.
4. Demoralization of the civil population of London and its provinces.
5. Progressive weakening of Britain's forces.

The plan drew on the doctrine contained in LDv 16 and some of the proposals made during September. The heart of the directive lay in the ambitions contained within points 2, 3 and 4, each of which were long-term objectives. The weather was worsening as winter approached and, with Hitler determined to begin a new campaign in the east in 1941, time was not on the Luftwaffe's side.

The first parachute landmines were probably dropped over London on the night of 16/17 September. Photographed on 19 September, this example has descended into a back garden in a London suburb – a testament to the inaccuracy of the Luftwaffe in general and the *luftmine* in particular. (Popperfoto/ Contributor, Getty)

Luftflotten 2 and 3 therefore took advantage of the cessation of major daylight attacks and the full moon period in mid-October to renew the campaign. Home Security reports noted a 'drift' in the bombing towards the centre of London during October, as the focus moved to Whitehall and the main railway stations.

The raids made increased use of parachute landmines. The first had been employed on the night of 16/17 September, when 12 were dropped by the minelaying specialists of KGr 126, probably in an attempt to disrupt shipping in the Port of London. Their use confirmed in the minds of many that the Luftwaffe was indulging in indiscriminate bombing. An outraged Churchill demanded retaliation in kind. Although the Air Staff was reluctant to acquiesce to the Prime Minister's demands, the Luftwaffe's increasing use of parachute landmines during September and October pushed Bomber Command nearer the policy of area bombing. The destructive power of the incendiary had not been fully realized at this stage. The number of incendiaries dropped actually declined from September to October. Frequent spells of cloud and rain in October and November caused increasingly scattered bombing. Some Luftwaffe crews, frustrated in their attempts to locate their primary objectives, resorted to secondary targets, or simply jettisoned their bombs at random.

Minor raids (in which less than 100 tons of high explosive (HE) was dropped) during the entire campaign against London were on a small scale. During September, Liverpool was raided 15 times. In October, in line with Göring's earlier directive, minor attacks were more frequent and flown by greater numbers of aircraft on Liverpool, Manchester, Birmingham and Coventry. Despite the frequently poor visibility, the number of *Störangriffen* raids fell from 420 in September to only 21 in October.

For both sides, the campaign on London underwent little variation. A typical example is the raid of 15 October, when Luftflotten 2 and 3 used fine visibility and a full moon to make a major joint attack on the capital. Approximately 410 bombers (some units flew two sorties) reported over London, with the majority bombing between 1900 and 2000 hours. To keep London under alert as long as possible, the last bombers did not leave until 0400 the following morning. Luftflotte 2's aircraft approached by two routes: the first between the Thames Estuary and Harwich, the other between Beachy Head and Dungeness. Luftflotte 3's aircraft, some no doubt using *Knickebein*, made landfall between Bognor Regis and Newhaven. The attack was opened by the He 111s of III/KG 26 and the 'fire lighters' of II/ KG 55. Approximately 538 tons of HE was dropped, the largest amount to date, together with 177 containers of incendiaries. Luftwaffe crews reported many fires in the eastern and central areas of London, with some stating the fires were the biggest they had yet seen.

The raid made comparatively little use of incendiaries but was severe in its effects. The Kennington Park Shelter, a trench lined with pre-cast concrete, was struck by an SC 250 which left 47 people dead. The worst incident occurred when a parachute mine descended on Dame Alice Owen's School in Edmonton, collapsing the building and blocking access to the basement in which some 150 people were sheltering. The blast wave ruptured a New

Piccadilly, London, 14 October 1940. The Luftwaffe struck the capital with renewed vigour during the full moon period in mid-October. The burning buildings, tangled hoses and silhouetted firemen remain some of the most powerful evocations of the Blitz. (Mirrorpix/Contributor, Getty)

OPPOSITE THE LONDON BLITZ, SEPTEMBER–NOVEMBER 1940

Between 7 September and 13 November 1940, the Luftwaffe made 67 raids on London and dropped 13,651 tons of high explosive bombs, as well as hundreds of thousands of incendiaries. The most heavily bombed area was from Waterloo Bridge to the loop of the Thames. Much of the bombing to the west and north of this area (Westminster, Marylebone and St Pancras) came later in the campaign, as the offensive spread across the government area and transport network hubs. The total area damaged testifies to the low level of bombing accuracy which characterized the London Blitz.

River culvert, which flooded the basement and killed many of the occupants. In addition, the damage caused a serious water shortage in a large area of London.

Although roads, railways and utilities were affected by the raid, service on most was partially restored relatively quickly. Industrial production was not, as a consequence, badly affected. The dock area received some damage and there was a major fire in warehouses and a grain store at the Royal Victoria Docks. Twenty-one parachute mines were reported, of which 12 did not explode. The bombing killed 213 people – the majority in the disaster at Dame Alice Owen's School – and injured 915.

In addition, more than 49 aircraft of Luftflotte 3 made minor raids on targets in the south and south-west, including the Westland factory at Yeovil and the Bristol works at Filton. Many of these raids failed to find their targets and bombs were scattered across the surrounding areas. A Focke-Wulf Fw 200 of KG 40 made a rare appearance over Britain in an unsuccessful attack on the Rolls-Royce factory at Hillington near Glasgow. The most damaging of these minor raids was that by 20 He 111s of KGr 100 on Birmingham.

Unverified claims were submitted by a Defiant crew from 264 Sqn and by a Blenheim of 23 Sqn. Despite Luftwaffe reports of intense searchlight activity, both interceptions were made using the light of the moon. AA Command made a single claim, which may have been a Junkers Ju 88 of LG 1. An interesting feature of the night was the Luftwaffe's 'Intruder' operations against those airfields which lay close to the flightpaths of the bombers. The attacks were clearly an attempt to hinder night-fighter operations.

The campaign against London lasted 67 nights, encompassing 57 major and ten minor raids. Approximately 13,351 tons of high explosive bombs were delivered over the course of the 57 major attacks. Overall, although profoundly tragic in many ways, the attacks were not as effective as either the Luftwaffe hoped or the British feared. The Luftwaffe failed to fulfil Göring's stated intention of the progressive and complete annihilation of London or to demoralize the civil population.

A chief factor was London's size. The Metropolitan Police area covered 700 square miles, the docklands area nine square miles. By contrast, in 1939 Berlin covered approximately 341 square miles and Paris just 40.5 square miles. London was enormous and easily absorbed the Luftwaffe's punishment. During September and October, the London Civil Defence region recorded 10,480 people killed and another 37,768 injured – a figure which, although serious, was considerably lower than pre-war estimates. That is not to say that the city remained completely unaffected and there were many notable tragedies. On 13 October, a large bomb or parachute mine penetrated a basement shelter in Stoke Newington, leading to at least 157 deaths. The following night, a 1,400kg bomb killed 67 people in the Balham Tube disaster. On 25 October, a 50kg bomb was enough to cause over 100 deaths in an infamous incident in the Druid Street Arches. A 1,400kg bomb struck Sloane Square Station on 12 November, where it penetrated the floor of the booking hall before exploding. A train below was crushed by falling debris, the building itself wrecked and 37 people killed. These were just some of the tragedies which took place during the London Blitz.

The shortage of public shelters caused many to seek whatever safety they could. The use of the Underground was opposed by the government at first but force of circumstance left it with no choice but to acquiesce. In October, official estimates put the number of

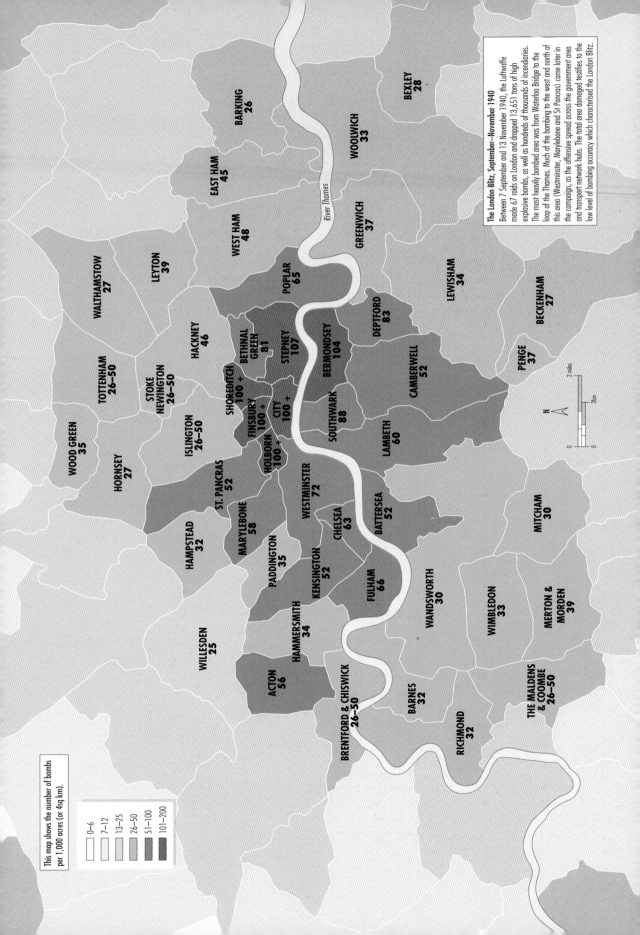

BARKING
26

BEXLEY
28

WOOLWICH
33

EAST HAM
45

WEST HAM
48

GREENWICH
37

LEWISHAM
34

BECKENHAM
27

River Thames

WALTHAMSTOW
27

LEYTON
39

POPLAR
65

DEPTFORD
83

PENGE
37

HACKNEY
46

BETHNAL
GREEN
81

STEPNEY
107

BERMONDSEY
104

CAMBERWELL
52

TOTTENHAM
26–50

STOKE
NEWINGTON
26–50

SHOREDITCH
100 +

FINSBURY
100 +

CITY
100 +

SOUTHWARK
88

LAMBETH
60

WOOD GREEN
35

ISLINGTON
26–50

HOLBORN
100 +

HORNSEY
27

ST. PANCRAS
52

WESTMINSTER
72

MITCHAM
30

MARYLEBONE
58

HAMPSTEAD
32

PADDINGTON
35

CHELSEA
63

BATTERSEA
52

KENSINGTON
52

FULHAM
66

WANDSWORTH
30

WIMBLEDON
33

MERTON &
MORDEN
39

N

2 miles

2 km

WILLESDEN
25

HAMMERSMITH
34

ACTON
56

BRENTFORD & CHISWICK
26–50

BARNES
32

RICHMOND
32

THE MALDENS
& COOMBE
26–50

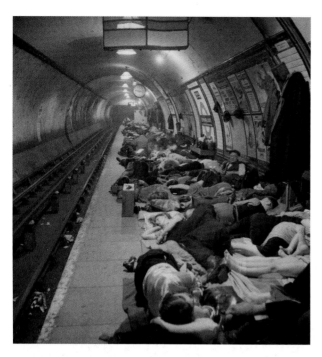

The Elephant and Castle underground station, November 1940. The numbers using the Tube every night may have been as high as 150,000. No beds, poor sanitation and hundreds of frightened people meant many chose to stay in their own homes for a few hours of decent sleep. (IWM/Getty Images/Contributor)

civilians sleeping each night in the Tube at 120,000. Others have put the figure even higher, at 150,000. Another 220,000, it was thought, were using public shelters of various types, railway arches and tunnels. Experience with public shelters, especially those built above ground, revealed serious problems. Some brick shelters, due to bureaucratic misunderstanding, were not built with Portland cement but with porous and weaker lime mortar. These shelters were death traps and hundreds of lives were lost as a consequence. Poor sanitation and lack of sleeping facilities caused much distress and steps were taken to improve conditions as the campaign went on. A public survey completed in November 1940 showed that only 40 per cent of Londoners sought refuge each night. The rest went to work as usual (war production continued at night) or simply stayed at home.

The damage to London's economy was severe but not fatal. The initial concentration on the dock area resulted in 21,000 gross tons (GT) of shipping being sunk and 48,000 GT damaged in the first three days. The warehouses, stores, yards and their stocks, which burned so brilliantly on the evening of 7 September, were destroyed in large quantities. Yet the vast network of quays, basins, gates, cranes and railway lines survived the Blitz largely intact. After the first raids, food stocks and other supplies were dispersed 'in buffer' to depots away from the docks. In any case, the Port of London handled a much-reduced volume of arrivals after June 1940, when the fall of France had rendered the approaches to the east coast ports vulnerable to E-boats, mines and aircraft.

The bombing caused delays and confusion on the railway network in and around London. Many of the lines south of the Thames were at times rendered unusable. The link lines between the northern and southern railway networks were damaged, seriously reducing the

London's railways were a principal target for the Luftwaffe and there were 667 hits on the railways in the capital alone during the first three weeks of the Blitz. Serious delays resulted and top priority was given to repairing damaged sections of track. (Popperfoto/Contributor, Getty)

flow of trains. For example, the London and North Eastern Railway normally forwarded 50 to 60 trains to the Southern Railway every day but there was a period when it was possible to forward only four trains to the Southern through London. Between 7 and 30 September, there were 667 hits on the railways, the majority in the London area. Priority was given to the clearing and repair of damaged sections of track, but unexploded bombs caused the worst delays. During September, between 5,000 and 6,000 railway wagons stood idle while UXBs were removed. Minor attacks across the country, especially those on Liverpool and Crewe, affected the rail network as delays created congestion in the goods yards.

It was estimated that about one bomb in 18 severed a gas, electricity or water main in London and 4,124 water mains were broken between September and November. Mindful of civilian morale and the risk of an epidemic, repair to public utilities was given high priority, though often hindered by debris which was difficult to clear. A Special Commissioner was appointed to the London Civil Defence region to coordinate salvage, clearance and repair of utilities and roads.

The first weeks of the Blitz created social chaos, as pre-war plans put in place by local authorities buckled under the strain. The bombing flooded ARP rest centres, which had been originally envisaged as brief stopover points for people emerging from shelters before they returned home. By 25 September, 25,590 people were residing in these temporary centres, most of them with nowhere to go. By early December, 32,160 houses had been demolished or damaged beyond repair and another commissioner was appointed to tackle the housing of the thousands made homeless. Charitable bodies as well as central government moved quickly to maintain social cohesion. A relief fund, established on 10 September, had raised £1,700,000 by mid-December.

The effect on civilian morale was greatest after the initial shock in mid-September. A Home Intelligence report of 9 September stated that, 'the strongest feeling [is] one of shock amongst all classes and in all districts as people have lulled themselves into a state of false security saying: "London is the safest place", and "they'll never get through the London defences"'. On 14 September, a German source (in fact the Military Attaché in Washington) stated that the campaign was seriously affecting morale in London. His report went on to claim that no fewer than 24 docks and four gasometers were destroyed, with serious damage to the railway stations at 'Sherrycross' and Waterloo. A report from the Ministry of Home Security claimed the opposite: 'The German attack upon London has had no fundamental ill effect either upon the capital or on the nation.' Later results were, from the German point of view, disappointing. In the first three months of the Blitz, the London region recorded just over two cases a week of what was described as 'bomb neuroses'.

Nor did class and racial divisions flare into outright violence. On 14/15 September, about 100 people, led by the Stepney Communist leader Peter Piratin, demanded admission to the Savoy Hotel's basement. Permission was reluctantly given and the night passed with no further incident. The episode, widely reported by American journalists who were present, stoked false hopes in Germany of political upheaval induced by the bombing. With little

It was said that the King and Queen were booed in London on 8 September. On 13 September, a bomb hit part of Buckingham Palace. The royal couple were now sharing the ordeal of their people and are seen visiting a bombed area the day after the palace was hit. (Fox Photos/ Stringer, Getty)

effective means of actively countering the Blitz, Churchill boosted morale by visiting the dock area on 8 September. A similar visit was made the following day by the King and Queen. The diarist Harold Nicolson recorded that the visit was booed but, on 13 September, a bomb wrecked the Royal Chapel at Buckingham Palace. The egalitarian nature of the bombing served, for the most part, to solidify the nation's unity.

The British defences

One of the Luftwaffe's campaign aims was to reduce its losses. In this, it was successful. In Lt Gen Pile's words, AA Command's Fixed Azimuth System, based on sound location of enemy bombers, 'broke down completely', when it was either swamped or bypassed altogether by the bombers on the opening nights of the Blitz. Pile moved swiftly in an attempt to improve AA Command's record. By 9 September, the number of guns defending London had been doubled and, the following day, Pile requested that no night-fighter patrols be flown over the London Inner Artillery Zone. The guns, given a free hand, proceeded to fire a Box Barrage over the city. Their 'largely wild and uncontrolled shooting' failed to destroy any bombers but the volume of noise generated by the barrage buoyed spirits in the embattled city. On 26/27 September, Pile instituted geographical barrages in an effort to reduce ammunition expenditure.

While AA Command's efforts may have encouraged those on the ground, one member of the Tizard Committee, Professor A.V. Hill, cogently expressed his opinion of AA Command's contribution. Hill observed that, as one cubic mile of space contains 5,451,776,000 cubic yards and the explosion of a 3.7in. shell covered a few thousand cubic yards for around one-fiftieth of a second, the idea of an effective barrage was misleading. To have even the slightest chance of hitting an aircraft would require thousands of shells to be fired every second. Over September, 260,000 shells were fired, for the destruction of fewer than a dozen German aircraft.

Fighter defence

During September and October, only seven bombers were shot down by night fighters – a performance worse than that of AA Command. For the RAF's Blenheims, taking-off and landing safely was more dangerous than the rare and often fruitless engagements with German bombers. Typical is the entry in 29 Sqn's ORB for 25 September 1940: 'Two bandits were chased using AI apparatus, but Blenheim was too slow.'

The Air Council searched desperately for a solution. While the GCI system remained in development, the first attempt to provide radar-controlled interception over land, the 'Kenley Experiment', was tried. Ten GL radar sets were 'borrowed' from AA Command and relocated at searchlight posts in the Kenley Sector. The contacts from the sets were passed to the Kenley Sector Operations Room, which could then provide the (approximate) height and bearing of the contact to the searchlights and the nearest night fighter. In theory, the searchlight beams could then guide the fighter in the right direction.

The experiment never really worked. The position of the night fighter was determined through radio direction-finding and the respective locations of the bomber and the interceptor were sometimes confused. Another problem was the lacklustre performance of the Blenheims of 600 and 219 Sqns, which carried out most of the patrols. The Beaufighter Mk IF was also tried, but the brand-new fighter was mired in the problems which plagued its entry into service. The fighters flew from Redhill, a new airfield with 'primitive' facilities and a damp climate which affected the delicate AI equipment.

On 11 September, as AA Command was firing its wild Box Barrage into the London sky, the Minister of Aircraft Production, Lord Beaverbrook, received a paper on night defence. The author, Marshal of the Royal Air Force Sir John Salmond, was at that time

The RAF's night-fighter force could do little to impede the Blitz during the autumn and winter of 1940. Pilot Officer Peter Kells, the pilot of a Blenheim Mk IF of No 29 Squadron, climbs into the cockpit for another night patrol, Coleby Grange, Lincolnshire, October 1940. (IWM CH 1584 (AHB))

Director of Armament Production at Beaverbrook's Ministry. With his customary energy, Beaverbrook rapidly cleared the way for Salmond to chair an investigation into the entire night-fighter issue.

The Salmond enquiry first met on 16 September. Dowding was invited to attend the third and final meeting two days later. On 1 October, the new Night Air Defence Committee, chaired by the Prime Minister, considered the enquiry's findings. The important recommendations were:

1. Interceptions out to sea under CH guidance were to be continued, despite the previous lack of success.
2. The task of filtering information should be delegated to the Group Operations Rooms to speed the process of interception.
3. Special training for night-fighting crews was needed. The formation of 54 Operational Training Unit (OTU) was authorized. Eye tests were to be introduced to assist in the selection of pilots – although why this was not already being done is something of a mystery.
4. In future, night fighters would be expected to fly in bad weather conditions with the assistance of navigational aids which would be installed at airfields.

The production of the following items was prioritized:

1. 600 GL Mk I radar sets, plus accelerated development of the much-improved GL Mk II and Searchlight Control (SLC or 'Elsie') radar sets.
2. Accelerated production of AI Mk IV and the Beaufighter Mk IF.
3. Accelerated production of trial GCI equipment.

Dowding's reluctance to commit day fighter squadrons to the night battle in September and October 1940 and his increasingly terse replies to questions regarding night defence were usually interpreted by his colleagues as intransigence. On 21 October, he reluctantly agreed to assign three squadrons of Hurricanes to the dangerous night-fighter role. To be fair, Dowding's attitude was matched in the squadrons. The 87 Sqn ORB recorded that 'permanent night flying … was definitely not viewed with favour by the squadron', later

OPPOSITE THE BLITZ NATIONWIDE, AUGUST 1940–MAY 1941

London received the overwhelming majority of the Luftwaffe's effort during the Blitz. The capital suffered 85 major raids over the eight months, in which approximately 23,949 tons of high explosive was dropped.

From mid-November, the campaign broadened, concentrating on the inland towns and the southern ports. The focus shifted again in spring 1941 to the west and south-west coast ports. There were many minor attacks on towns and cities across Britain during the Blitz but the main weight remained on London and the ports.

The 15 remaining cities received 11,807 tons, less than half London's total. Nevertheless, comparatively small quantities of bombs could cause enormous damage to smaller cities, such as Coventry or Plymouth.

adding that it was 'not a popular move and to start with one and all were pretty "browned off"'… Charmy Down consisted of three good runways and plenty of mud'.

Salmond had already written to Churchill, pressing for Dowding to be replaced at Fighter Command. Finally, on 25 November, Dowding 'retired' and his place was taken by Sir William Sholto Douglas. None of the planned improvements to Britain's night defences would be ready in time for the next phase of the campaign. London's solo ordeal may have been almost at an end but the Luftwaffe was about to turn its attentions elsewhere.

The campaign on the Midlands and southern ports (14 November 1940–18 February 1941)

On 10 October 1940, the staff at the Luftwaffe's forward HQ (enigmatically codenamed 'Robinson') wrote a new intelligence appreciation of the campaign's progress. The report painted a sanguine picture:

- British airframe and engine manufacture was 'expected' to be reduced by 50 per cent.
- 1,770 RAF fighters had been destroyed between 1 July and 9 October.
- The London docks were largely destroyed.

The report was received by Major von Dewitz, a staff analyst in Berlin, with scepticism. A lack of photographs, he considered, prevented real assessment of damage. Moreover, the staff at Robinson were viewing things too optimistically. The campaign on London, he suggested, had reached a stalemate and he proposed the following course of action:

1. Shift the focus to the outer industrial areas of London.
2. Begin heavier raids on the industrial Midlands, in particular Coventry, Birmingham and Sheffield.
3. Make sudden shifts in the attack back to London.

Dewitz was not alone in his ideas. Attacks thus far on London had failed to cripple either its economy or the will of its inhabitants. Luftwaffe doctrine suggested that the next step was to prevent Fighter Command making good its losses by disabling the aircraft and engine industry. The towns of the Midlands offered greater opportunities for complete destruction, with associated effects on both industrial output and civilian morale. According to a Luftwaffe Intelligence note of 21 October, bombing of the industrial heartland would affect the 'well-to-do' British capitalists who formed the basis of the government's support. Central England was the home of the 'really stubborn' businessmen who formed the basis of the government's will to resist.

The aims of the next phase were therefore:
- To maintain the pressure on London through daylight *Jabo* (*Jagdbomber*: fighter-bomber) attacks and occasional heavy night raids.
- To begin a series of major attacks on the industrial Midlands by the light of the full moon.
- To intensify the anti-shipping campaign.

FRANCE

North Sea

English Channel

ENGLAND

London
Port & Centre of government
7 Sept–13 Nov, 15, 16, 29 Nov,
8, 27, 29 Dec, 11, 12 Jan,
8, 15, 19 Mar, 16, 19 Apr, 10 May

Hull
Port
18 Mar, 7, 8 May

Newcastle-Tyneside
Port
9 Apr

Sheffield
Steel & Armaments
12 Dec

Coventry
Aircraft & Vehicles
14 Nov, 8 Apr

Portsmouth
Naval base
10 Jan, 10 Mar, 17 Apr

Isle of Wight

Southampton
Port & Aircraft
17, 23, 30 Nov, 1 Dec

Bristol-Avonmouth
Port
24 Nov, 2 Dec, 3, 16 Jan,
16 Mar, 11 Apr

Manchester
Port & Aircraft industry
22, 23 Dec, 9 Jan

Birmingham
Steel, Armaments,
Aircraft & Vehicles
19, 20, 22 Nov,
3, 11 Dec, 11 Mar,
9, 10 Apr

Cardiff
Port
2 Jan

WALES

Liverpool-Birkenhead
Port & Shipbuilding
28–31 Aug, 28 Nov,
20, 21 Dec, 12 Mar,
26 Apr, 2, 3, 7 May

Isle of Man

Plymouth-Devonport
Naval base
20, 21 Mar, 21, 22, 23, 28, 29 Apr

SCOTLAND

Glasgow-Clydeside
Port & Shipbuilding
13, 14 Mar, 7 Apr, 5, 6 May

Irish Sea

Belfast
Shipbuilding
15 Apr, 4 May

NORTHERN
IRELAND

IRELAND

N

50 miles

50km

0

0

A heavily laden Heinkel He 111 takes off, reputedly on 1 March 1941. The very heavy *Satan* and *Max* bombs affected aircraft handling to such a degree that specially selected crews were chosen for the task of dropping them over the UK. (Keystone-France/Contributor, Getty)

The combination of distance, inclement weather and industrial haze increased the difficulty of bombing Britain's inland towns. The Luftwaffe aimed to overcome these problems in four ways.

Confidence in *Knickebein* had waned during October and November as No 80 Wing's jamming became more effective. Given clear weather, the nights between the first and last lunar quarters (and in particular the four nights on either side of the full moon) provided ideal conditions for visual bombing. The Luftwaffe had used the full moon period to good effect in October and planned to do so again in November and December. These periods of intensified activity became known as *Mondscheinserenaden* (Moonlight Serenades). However, the cloudless nights necessary for visual bombing could by no means be guaranteed during the winter months. Conversely, fine weather often produced fog and mist by early morning and prudence therefore dictated that the bombers be home in the early hours before landing conditions worsened.

In addition, the attacks would be led by the three specialist target-marking Gruppen. KGr 100 and III/KG 26 would employ large numbers of incendiaries, while II/KG 55 dropped a mixture of parachute flares, incendiaries and very heavy bombs, including the SC 1400 and SC 1800. RAF Signals Intelligence examined the Luftwaffe's radio traffic closely and correctly concluded that the leading KGr 100 aircraft transmitted weather reports as it crossed the English coast and again as it approached the target. After it had marked the target, the same aircraft might 'stooge' in the area, before overflying the target again to report the raid's progress.

The main force would carry increased numbers of heavier HE bombs, to blast open buildings and hinder firefighting by wrecking utilities. In January, the 2,500kg bomb ('Max') was introduced. A greater proportion of incendiaries than hitherto would be scattered over the area, where they would enter buildings and begin hundreds of fires.

Finally, by repeatedly attacking the same targets in individual 'Blitzes', the Luftwaffe aimed to overwhelm the smaller cities, slow the recovery of their industries and hamper the rebuilding of social cohesion.

Target *Korn*

Coventry was known as 'Britain's motor city'. The medieval streets and array of some 30 engineering works clustered in the centre made the city the best prospect for an annihilating blow. Coventry had already been attacked by KGr 100 and III/KG 26 several times in the ten days prior to the raid and both units made 'dry-runs' on 12/13 November. For the main attack, Luftflotten 2 and 3 would together dispatch 552 aircraft. The three beam

The first incendiary markers, dropped by KGr 100, fell to the east of Coventry's 14th century Cathedral Church of St Michael on the night of 14/15 November 1940. The cathedral was almost completely destroyed in the ensuing attack. Industrial production in the city was badly affected but not halted. (George W. Hales/Stringer, Getty)

systems were used but the fires which took hold early in the attack served as a beacon for the following aircraft.

In the days before 14 November, prisoner interrogations and intercepted wireless traffic which mentioned the word *Korn* (Grain) revealed that the Luftwaffe was planning a major attack. *Korn* was not recognized as the codename for Coventry. London was considered a possibility but the more probable target was a city in the Midlands. The detection of the beams over Coventry in the afternoon of 14 November made it apparent that the city was the target. In a decision much-debated since, no early warning was given to the city.

KGr 100 duly opened the attack at 1920hrs, when the first bombs were dropped just to the east of the cathedral. The 'Bromides' were tuned to the wrong frequency and, despite one being almost underneath KGr 100's flightpath, they failed to disturb the *X-Gerät* sets. The attacking force, employing the *Krokodil* tactic, gave the defences no respite. The bombing cut telephone lines at an early stage and communications inside and outside the city were affected. Water mains burst and the overwhelmed fire service resorted to using any sources of water they could find, including ponds and ornamental lakes. Smaller fires coalesced to form giant conflagrations. Although the bombing was concentrated on the city centre, many bombs were scattered around the industries – and housing – on the outskirts of Coventry. The attackers dropped a total of 535 tons of bombs in a mix of 94 per cent high explosive and 6 per cent incendiaries. The only success registered by the defences was a Dornier Do 17 of 6./KG 3, which crashed near Loughborough. The night's most famous casualty was the 14th-century Cathedral Church of St Michael. The bombing killed 554 people and seriously injured another 865.

The aerial reconnaissance images of Coventry, on which the Luftwaffe's post-raid assessment was based, were obscured by cloud and smoke. The analysis suggested that 12 factories were severely damaged and another eight were presumed to have suffered equal damage. Nazi propaganda portrayed *Mondscheinsonate* as revenge for Bomber Command's raid on Munich a few days earlier. Goebbels' Propaganda Ministry falsely attributed a new verb, *Coventriert* (to 'Coventrate'), to the British public.

A report prepared for the War Cabinet told another story. Production was 'entirely suspended' at only three major factories. Damage at four more was described as 'serious'. Several smaller works were badly damaged and one, the Triumph factory, was 'completely

KEY

- 🏭 factory
- AA gun
- ✝ cathedral
- ◆ fire station

▬	Luftflotte 2 and Luftflotte 3
▬	Luftflotte 2
▬	KGr 100
▬	Luftflotte 3
– – – – – –	beam

EVENTS

1 1910hrs. Air Raid Warning Red is issued to the Coventry Civil Defence command post. Minutes later, the first fires are reported as the *X-Gerät*-equipped Heinkel He 111s of KGr 100 arrive at three-and-a-half-minute intervals over the city centre. The first bombs fall around the city's cathedral.

2 2000hrs. Bombers of Luftflotte 2 begin to arrive from the north-east. They drop a mixture of incendiary and high explosive bombs, damaging the gas and water mains and cutting electricity and telephone lines.

3 As a consequence, Coventry's civil defence nerve centre is almost completely cut off. Meanwhile, the city's firemen are forced to fall back on whatever sources of water are available. Firefighting reinforcements start to arrive but the defenders are already fighting a losing battle.

4 2015hrs. More aircraft from Luftflotte 2 and Luftflotte 3 arrive from the south. Incendiaries fall outside the burning city centre and fires begin to develop simultaneously in widely separated areas. With the communications system in disarray, the Fire Service is unable to respond efficiently. Fires join together to produce conflagrations.

5 The active defences are ineffective. In an unusual move, some of Coventry's AA guns are re-sited to the city centre in Broadgate and Pool Meadow.

6 2300hrs. The main force from Luftflotte 3 begins to arrive. Among the units detailed to specified targets are: KGr 606: Cornercraft and the Hill Street gasworks. II/KG 27: the Alvis factory. III/KG 55: the large Daimler plant. I/LG 1: the Standard Cars buildings at Canley. I/KG 51: the British Piston Ring works.

7 The raid continues through the night, the last bombers not leaving until 0535hrs. Combined with the clear moonlit night and the feeble defences, the bombers have had no difficulty in finding their target. Crews report the centre and eastern part of the city as being a 'sea of flames'.

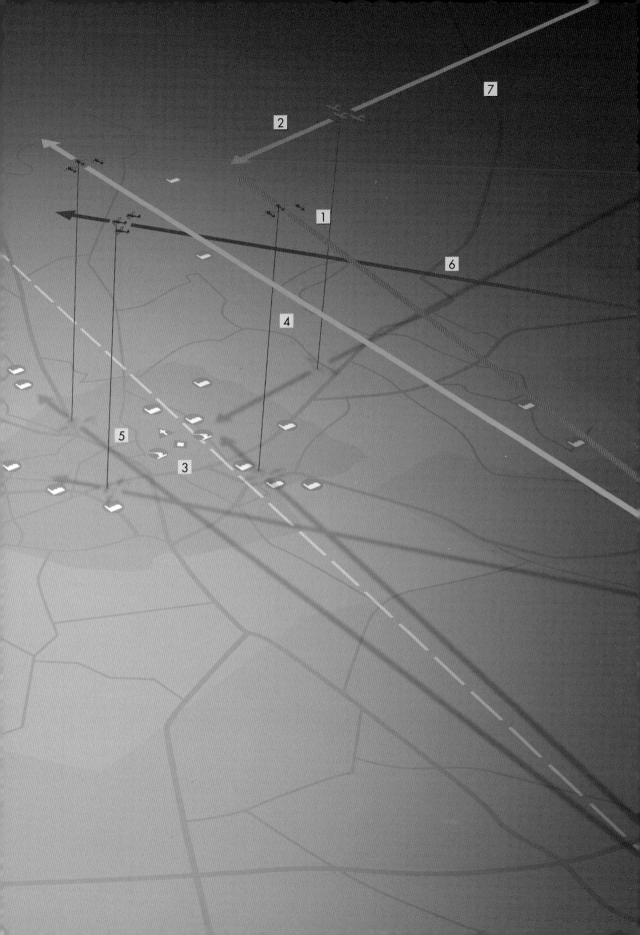

gutted'. Industrial production was most affected, not by bomb or fire damage but by the disruption to gas, water and electricity supplies. By 18 November, the city had made a surprising recovery: electricity production was restored to 50 per cent, the water supply was mostly reinstated, telephone lines were under repair, the majority of UXBs defused and all but one railway line was back in operation.

Morale was shaken but seemed to recover quickly. A Home Intelligence document reported, 'During Friday [15 November] there was great depression, a widespread feeling of impotence and many open signs of hysteria.' By 16 November, in anticipation of a follow-up raid, the police organized transport out of the city for up to 10,000 people. Only 300 citizens are estimated to have left Coventry that evening – although more did so unofficially. A visit by the King, the War Cabinet report stated, had 'a remarkably steadying and cheering effect … of incalculable value'.

Firemen fight a burning building in Manchester. Almost 70 tons of incendiaries were dropped during the two attacks on Manchester in December 1940, destroying large areas of the city centre. However, apart from a third attempt in January, Manchester was not hit by a major raid again. (IWM/Getty Images)

Regenschirm: The Birmingham Blitz

Birmingham was a significant industrial centre. Apart from the various iron and steel works, Austin, Birmingham Small Arms (BSA), Dunlop, Lucas, Rootes, Singer (mistaken by the Luftwaffe for the sewing machine company), Sunbeam and Wolesley had a major presence in the city. Rover (manufacturing Bristol Hercules engines) was based at Solihull.

The Luftwaffe launched major raids on 19/20, 20/21 and 22/23 November against *Regenschirm* ('Umbrella': a reference to Birmingham's most famous son, Neville Chamberlain). A fourth attack came on 11/12 December and minor raids were dispatched on 3/4 and 4/5 December. In a bid to ensure accuracy, III/KG 26 assisted in target-marking in all six attacks and KGr 100 on five. Although visibility was good on 19/20 November, only 356 out of 439 aircraft dispatched bombed the target. Poor weather compromised the attacks of 20/21 November and 11/12 December. The most successful raid was that of 22/23 November, when all three target-marking Gruppen arrived simultaneously and a high level of concentration was achieved. Visibility was good and within one and a half hours, fires could be seen by crews approaching from the south coast.

Altogether, in the course of four major and two minor raids, 1,067 bombers reported over the target and dropped a total of 1,171 tons of high explosive and 104 tons of incendiaries. The opening raid on 19/20 November hit the BSA factory at Small Heath, killing 50 employees working on the night shift. The attack on 22/23 November lasted 11 hours and hit 72 factories. Yet, only four were 'severely' damaged while 55 received 'slight' or 'negligible' damage. Overall, Birmingham's industry was not badly affected by the bombing. As in Coventry, the greatest industrial dislocation came from shortages of gas and electricity.

'Crucible': Sheffield

The third of the trio of industrial cities selected by the Luftwaffe was Sheffield, which for obvious reasons received the codename *Schmelztiegel* ('Crucible'). The heart of Britain's steel industry, the north-east part of the city was dominated by iron and steel works, coking plants and armaments factories.

It was therefore this area of the city which formed the *Schwerpunkt* (Concentration Point) for the attack on 12/13 December. Although the weather was favourable, only 336 out of 406 (83 per cent) crews claimed to find Sheffield. The majority – 270 – came from Luftflotte 3.

The attack was opened by II/KG 55 but, despite their efforts, concentration was poor. The force scattered bombs across north-east England and numerous incidents were reported all over the country. The tram network was most badly affected. Every tramcar in the city centre sustained damage and some of the overhead wires were destroyed.

Three nights later, Luftflotten 2 and 3 tried again. Poor weather blunted the attack and two Gruppen were instructed while en route to attack secondary targets. Of the 94 aircraft remaining, only 77 claimed to have reached Sheffield.

The two attacks killed 589 people and seriously injured another 488. Industrial damage was regarded as superficial. It was very difficult to destroy coke ovens and heavy steel-making industrial plants with the bombs at the Luftwaffe's disposal, and the greatest damage was caused by fire. As was the case in Coventry and Birmingham, the Luftwaffe's assessment was not matched by results.

The Luftwaffe sought to balance the campaign between industry and the major ports during November and December: there were three major attacks against Liverpool, two on Bristol and one on Plymouth. The most devastating were the back-to-back raids on Liverpool, made in fine visibility during the moon's last quarter, on 20/21 and 21/22 December. The actual impact on Merseyside was not as great as the Luftwaffe assumed. The vast dock area absorbed the punishment and the Cabinet report noted that, while a good deal of produce was lost, 'generally speaking, the working of the Port has not been seriously affected'. Luftflotte 3's efforts against Bristol did little to damage the flow of goods through the port. Although the attack on Plymouth naval base was unsuccessful, with the majority of bombs falling into the sea or in open countryside, this port was to suffer much worse in the months to come.

The Manchester Blitz

The Greater Manchester area's importance to the Luftwaffe lay with the Manchester Ship Canal, connecting Salford with Liverpool, and the aviation and armaments industries in Manchester and Trafford Park. The first attack, made on 22/23 December, benefited by guidance from the fires still burning in Liverpool from the raids of the two previous nights. The attacks were led by KGr 100 and II/KG 55, which succeeded in marking the centre of Manchester on both nights. The very serious fires which resulted put a heavy strain on Manchester's fire service, which had assisted in Liverpool on the two previous nights. Trafford Park received considerable punishment the following night, when 13 Avro Manchesters were destroyed on the Metropolitan-Vickers production line.

The *X-Gerät* revealed

Birmingham was attacked by two aircraft of KGr 100 on the night of 6/7 November 1940. One was Heinkel He 111H-2, 6N+BH, flown by Feldwebel Hans Lehmann. After reaching the target, the aircraft turned for home, whereupon it suffered compass failure. Lehmann therefore tuned the radio compass to the transmitter at St Malo. When the aircraft passed over the radio beacon, the pilot descended through the cloud but found himself over the sea. Imagining the aircraft was now over the Bay of Biscay, Lehmann reversed course, hoping to find the Brittany coast. By now low on fuel, a coastline was sighted and Lehmann chose to force land on the beach. He misjudged his approach and the He 111 came down in the surf. One crewman was killed and the surviving crew members waded ashore.

The aircraft was in fact off West Bay, Bridport. Lehmann had tuned the compass to an RAF Masking Beacon, or 'Meacon', at Templecombe in Dorset. An army detachment began the He 111's recovery the next day. A naval vessel then arrived, the commander of which insisted on taking charge. The ship towed the He 111 into deeper water and prepared to begin the salvage. The line then broke and the aircraft sank to the bottom. 'It is a very great pity', wrote an exasperated Professor Lindemann to Churchill, 'that inter-Service squabbles resulted in the loss of this machine, which is the first of its kind to come within our grasp'.

The Heinkel was recovered some days later and the *X-Gerät* equipment taken to Farnborough for examination. It was later claimed that the discovery of the *X-Gerät* secrets assisted 80 Wing in countering the X-beam. However, later research by Alfred Price revealed that the countermeasures, under the codename 'Bromide', were not especially successful.

The King visits Southampton, 5 December 1940. There were reports of the royal party and attendant local officials being booed. The Bishop of Winchester thought the city 'broken in spirit'. Yet there was no solid evidence of 'defeatism' and the Luftwaffe did not bomb Southampton in strength again after 1 December. (Keystone/ Stringer, Getty)

The two raids were notable for the destruction of a vast amount of housing, leaving 10,000 people in Manchester, Salford and Stretford homeless. The actual loss of production was regarded as small. On 9/10 January, Manchester received its third and final major raid. In deteriorating weather conditions, a large number of bombers were compelled to seek secondary targets and only 143 aircraft claimed to bomb Manchester. The bombing achieved no concentration, and damage to vital key points was minor.

The Southampton Blitz

The attraction of Southampton (codenamed *Markthalle* or Market Hall) as a target lay not only in its importance as a commercial port but also in its proximity to Luftflotte 3's airfields. Recourse to full use of *X*- or *Y-Gerät* beams for target-marking was considered unnecessary and on the first three nights the assault was opened by II/KG 55. Possibly due to scattered bombing, the fourth and final attack was opened by III/KG 26, with the other specialist Gruppen acting as back-up. There was a 13 per cent failure to find the target across the four attacks, in contrast to the 17–18 per cent of sorties which failed to bomb Coventry, Birmingham and Sheffield.

The first major raid came on 17/18 November, two nights after the moon was at its fullest. Thick cloud impeded target identification, bombs were scattered all over the town and the docks suffered little damage. The raid on 23/24 November likewise produced little result. The last two attacks were the most damaging. On the night of 30 November/1 December, the bombing concentrated on the city centre. Water mains were damaged, greatly hampering efforts to fight the fires. A follow-up raid the next night was made in clear visibility but curtailed by the risk of early morning fog at Luftflotte 3's airfields. Ten large unextinguished fires were still burning from the previous night, and returning crews commented on the extensive flames which appeared to cover the north and west of the target. The shortage of water was again a problem. The Thorneycroft and Supermarine works were both damaged but industry on the whole was little affected.

The dock area, the intended target of the four attacks, escaped with only minor damage. Much of the bombing concentrated on the city centre, where public utilities were badly

The fires in London's dockland cast a glow on the horizon, November 1940. Although the Luftwaffe switched its attention to the industrial towns and the ports, London remained an important target. (ullstein bild Dtl./Contributor, Getty)

affected. This factor, combined with a perception of local official ineptitude, may have contributed to the perceived slump in morale.

London campaign renewed

The Luftwaffe's main target remained London. Between 14 November and the end of the year, the capital received 1,523 tons of high explosive and 222 tons of incendiaries in six major raids. The *Schwerpunkt* on each occasion was *Zielraum Otto* (Target Area O), encompassing the City and Whitehall. The largest attacks were made on 15/16 November (*Mondscheinserenade Loge*) and 8/9 December. The latter was the heaviest raid then attempted, with the exception of Coventry. A massive quantity of incendiaries, almost 115 tons, was dropped: 23 per cent of the total. Extensive damage was caused in the docklands. Fifty people are thought to have lost their lives when a parachute mine detonated between the Langham Hotel and Broadcasting House.

Marking time: January and February 1941

Optimistic Luftwaffe assessments, together with wild underestimates of British airframe and engine production for 1941, could not disguise a growing feeling that the best way to continue the Blitz was by concentrating on the long-term counter-blockade. On 17 November, State Secretary Ernst von Weizsäcker confirmed that, despite the apparent success against Coventry, greater potential was offered by a blockade and the possibility of starvation among the British population.

New instructions issued on 13 January by OKW stated that the attacks against the industrial cities of Britain were to be scaled down in favour of an all-out night-time assault on the most important harbours, the approaches to which were to be mined. However, key points of the air armaments and aircraft industry were still to be subjected, whenever possible, to *Störangriffen* raids during daylight hours.

All this was easier said than done. Poor winter weather created unsuitable flying conditions and waterlogged airfields. The Luftwaffe would make just seven major raids in January and none at all in February. The opportunity was taken during this relative inactivity to reshuffle some of the Kampfgeschwader. Fliegerkorps X was re-formed in

Sicily with the following elements: 2./KG 4, II/KG 26 and II and III/LG 1. After a dispiriting campaign, the CAI withdrew from Belgium in mid-January, to prepare for operations in the Mediterranean. Conditions were no better for the RAF. The 604 Sqn ORB between 20 and 31 January records nothing except 'No flying. FOG' and 'No flying. Mist and bad visibility'.

The new year was marked by the Luftwaffe on 2/3 January, when Cardiff received its heaviest raid of the Blitz. Led by KGr 100, 111 aircraft conducted a two-phase attack on the dock area and the large steelworks located in the south-east of the town. A decoy site at Leckwith attracted a number of bombs and the well-prepared Civil Defences had extinguished most of the town's fires by midnight.

Three attacks against Bristol/Avonmouth on 3/4, 4/5 and 16/17 January were largely ineffective, with no real concentration achieved. The first two raids were marred by the late arrival of KGr 100, which forced aircraft from the main force to circle while waiting for the target to be marked. The Bristol fire service demonstrated real efficiency: on 3/4 January, they struggled with water freezing in the hoses but extinguished the fires so quickly on the following night that some bomber crews became confused and attacked Weston-super-Mare instead.

Two major raids on London on 11/12 and 12/13 January were compromised by deteriorating weather at the airfields in France. The first attack was considered the more serious. The second did not receive the benefit of proper target-marking and KGr 100 bombed by dead reckoning through a thick cloud base. The raid of 11/12 January achieved notoriety when at least 55 people were killed after a bomb penetrated the booking hall at Bank underground station. The resulting crater, said to be the largest in London, was not repaired until May.

Firestorm. The tangle of narrow medieval streets which made up the City proved perfect for the Luftwaffe's raid on the night of 29/30 December 1940. The low tide of the Thames hindered efficient firefighting. The results were catastrophic. (Hulton Archive/Stringer, Getty)

'Mutton', Free balloon barrages, Intruders and GCI

The winter of 1940–41 saw Fighter Command continue to struggle with the vexed issue of night defence. Fighters made only 13 claims between November and February.

One solution was an idea for an 'aerial minefield' to be sown in the path of approaching bombers. The first aircraft chosen was the Handley Page Harrow, an obsolete bomber which took 40 minutes to reach its stated ceiling of 19,200ft and had an (optimistic) maximum speed of 190mph. The far more capable Havoc was used later in the campaign.

When dropped from the aircraft, the mine opened a parachute. Attached to the base was 2,000ft of wire with a second, unopened parachute. A Harrow dropped 120 mines at 200ft intervals, producing a 'curtain' four and a half miles long and half a mile deep. The mines fell at around 1,000ft per minute and so, if released at 20,000ft, remained effective for about ten minutes. When an aircraft struck a wire, the shock severed a weak link holding the upper parachute. As this broke away, a small stabilizing parachute was deployed. The same shock also released the parachute at the other end of the wire. The forward speed of the aircraft, acting against the drag of the parachutes, caused the bomb to be pulled down onto the aircraft and explode. All this relied on a good deal of happy circumstance.

Known as the Long Aerial Mine (LAM), the scheme received the RAF name 'Mutton', which says everything. The idea did, however, enjoy the support of Churchill's scientific adviser and confidant, Professor Frederick Lindemann. Amazingly, Mutton may have scored two successes and it was December 1941, long after the Blitz had ended, before it was finally abandoned.

A similar idea which gained some traction in the late winter of 1940/41 was the 'free balloon barrage', at first known as 'Pegasus' and later as 'Albino'. This entailed the release of a number of free-floating barrage balloons, each equipped with 'a lethal charge' into the expected path of enemy bombers. The plan naturally would not work if wind scattered the balloons out of the area in which it was expected the bombers would arrive. Perhaps surprisingly, free balloon barrages were launched more than once. The first attempt, on 27/28 December, resulted in a large number of mysterious explosions across the south-east of England. On no occasion were any enemy aircraft destroyed and balloons were sometimes last seen drifting over France.

A more sensible concept was the 'Intruder' operation, pioneered by the Blenheims of 600 and 604 Sqns in June 1940. Improvements in Y-Service interception and decryption of Luftwaffe signals traffic meant that Fighter Command HQ would have an idea of which bomber units were to be operating on a given night. In December, therefore, the Blenheims of 23 Sqn were stripped of their secret AI equipment for attacks on German bombers as they departed and arrived at their airfields. The Blenheims were also equipped with flares and bombs for attacks on the airfields themselves. The perennial problem of the Blenheim's slow speed did not matter as much when attacking bombers 'in the circuit,' but definite kills remained few and far between. In March 1941, the Hurricanes of 87 Sqn were detailed for Intruder operations. In the following month, 23 Sqn received the first Douglas Havoc Mk I (Intruder), which offered a considerable improvement in performance over the Blenheim. The operations began slowly and not altogether successfully: three Intruders were lost between December and February, and it was March before any claims were made. More success would follow, however, and RAF Intruder operations would continue for the rest of the war.

The first Ground Controlled Interception stations were not without their teething problems. GCI could not gauge heights of contacts accurately. This problem was solved

Tenente Pietro Affiani, 243 Squadriglia, 99 Gruppo, is escorted through Liverpool Street Station on 11 November 1940. His Fiat BR 20 had been shot down a few hours earlier by Hurricanes over Suffolk and two of the crew of six killed. (Central Press/ Stringer Getty)

The Second Great Fire of London

On 29/30 December, 136 aircraft from Luftflotten 2 and 3, led by KGr 100, targeted *Zielraum Otto* once again. At 1817hrs, the first bombs began to fall in the jumble of streets that made up the Square Mile. Despite the cloudy conditions, a high degree of concentration was obtained and 22,068 incendiaries were dropped – an incredible average of 114 per minute. The attack, curtailed by poor weather over French airfields, was over by 2130hrs. Here, a Junkers Ju 88A-1 of 5./KG54 is seen approaching the City during the last stages of the raid.

The City was left engulfed by six enormous conflagrations. Communications broke down when the Wood Street telephone exchange was gutted. To make matters worse, the Thames tide was at an abnormally low ebb, which greatly hampered the fire services. Those who were there remembered the searing air and a wind which carried sparks and burning embers from one building to the next. The firemen were forced back, as one street after another was set alight and the air became too hot to breathe. The raid had in fact created what can be described as a proto-firestorm. The 'Second Great Fire' destroyed or damaged many historic buildings, including the Guildhall. Eight Wren churches, ironically built in the redevelopment following the First Great Fire, perished in the flames. St Paul's famously – and miraculously – survived.

by linking the system to GL radar sets, which were able to give accurate height information. The GCI controller could only guide one interception at a time, although a later 'cab rank' system of having AI fighters airborne and ready was introduced.

The anti-aircraft contribution

The effectiveness of AA Command gradually improved, thanks to various small but significant changes. When the Luftwaffe shifted its attacks from London, a major redistribution of AA batteries followed. The GL Mk I set possessed a large blind spot at elevation angles of more than 45 degrees, meaning that aircraft could no longer be tracked as they passed overhead. In January 1941, therefore, the decision was taken to pass gun control back to the Gun Operations Rooms, where information from multiple GL sets could be used to compute firing solutions and passed to the batteries. In early 1941, the 'Search Light Control' radar (SLC, known colloquially as 'Elsie') began to be introduced in limited numbers to improve searchlight tracking. The apparatus was smaller and simpler than the GL Mk II sets and thus easier to produce in quantity. Elsie possessed a maximum detection range of eight miles and was mounted directly to a 150cm 'Master' searchlight.

Bank underground station was largely destroyed – and at least 55 people killed – on 11/12 January when a bomb exploded inside the booking hall. The blast wave collapsed the escalators 'like a pack of cards', blowing people from a platform under a moving train. The huge crater was not properly repaired until May. (Bentley Archive/Popperfoto/Contributor, Getty)

Bonito, Domino and Starfish

If interference with the *Knickebein* beams continued to produce results, efforts against *X-Gerät* were less effective. It was only after Coventry that examination of the Bridport Heinkel He 111 revealed the correct re-radiated note of *X-Gerät* and the Bromides began operating on the right setting. In addition, the *X-Gerät* alignments were occasionally received through Enigma decrypts, which helped considerably in second-guessing Luftwaffe intentions. Evidence accumulated over the winter of 1940–41 seemed to indicate that the accuracy formerly shown by KGr 100 had diminished and it was assumed that this was due to successful countermeasures by 80 Wing.

However, more recent evidence suggests that the radio operators of KGr 100 were not misled by the re-radiated signals from the Bromides. Instead, the lightweight incendiaries used by KGr 100 inevitably caused scattered target-marking. The bombers which followed the specialist pathfinders were subject to the same cloud and high winds, and the usual result was poor bombing concentration.

The first *Y-Gerät* transmissions (codenamed 'Bonito' by R.V. Jones) were heard by 80 Wing in November. When the transmissions were examined, it was found that there were separate signals to identify the aircraft's bearing and range from the ground station. The British countermeasure, codenamed 'Domino', used a receiver at Highgate, which sent the signal on to the powerful BBC transmitter at Alexandra Palace. The re-radiated signal went from there back to the *Y-Gerät* ground station, confusing both the system's range and direction.

Domino began transmitting in February 1941 and another station was soon established at Beacon Hill near Salisbury. On 9 March, the *Y-Gerät* signals suddenly changed in an unsuccessful attempt to shake off the jamming. Two days later, the Beacon Hill station was bombed with sufficient accuracy to put it off air for two days. British sources state that during the first half of March, only 18 aircraft of III/KG 26 received the bomb-release signal.

A scheme of day and night decoys for airfields and naval installations had been underway since July and a proposal to supply civil decoys for major towns was pushed forward as a priority. By 23 November, the first hurriedly constructed Special Fire (SF or 'Starfish') sites were in place outside Coventry and Birmingham. Starfish soon gained the personal backing of Churchill and, between December 1940 and June 1941, SF sites were opened at a rate of almost one a day around Britain.

The sites were situated five to ten miles from city centres and at least two miles from the suburbs. Considerable ingenuity was displayed by the sites' designers, many of whom had become experts at deceiving the eye during careers in the film-set industry. The sites had to be capable of being 'switched on' at a moment's notice, then to 'take' rapidly and burn for as long as the raid lasted. Decoy fires varied greatly and the design depended on the town or city they were guarding: some, made from steel and asbestos 'buildings' covered with tarred roofing felt, were designed to burn quickly. Other versions used various mixtures of coal, paraffin or creosote to produce different intensities and colours. Each Starfish site was made from a number of different decoy fires, the better to resemble a section of burning town. In theory, if a town's fire service could put out the early fires quickly, a lit Starfish site could easily attract the remainder of a night's bombing.

The Starfish proved their worth quickly: on 2/3 December, the site at Stockwood near Bristol drew several bombs during an attack led by KGr 100. Luftwaffe crew reports (which had already mentioned decoys during the Coventry raid) are peppered with references to fires seen on the approaches to targets. Not all SF sites were a success and some rarely, if ever, drew any bombs at all. Those situated on the outskirts of London were generally a failure due to the difficulty in decoying bombers away from such a large and obvious target. On the other hand, there would be some real successes for Starfish in the spring of 1941.

The government produced a vast number of posters, one of which exhorted citizens to 'Beat Firebomb Fritz'. The 1kg B1E1 incendiary proved the most destructive bomb of the Blitz. In the campaign on London between September and November 1940, Home Security estimated that one ton of incendiaries caused approximately 80 fires. (DEA / G. NIMATALLAH/ Contributor, Getty)

The destruction wrought by fire in December's attacks on Manchester and London led to Home Secretary Herbert Morrison's call for volunteer fire-watchers. These 'chorus girls' from Newcastle's Theatre Royal enjoy practising putting out a fire on the theatre's roof. (Keystone/Stringer, Getty)

OPPOSITE GCI

The Ground Controlled Interception (GCI) gradually became operational during the spring of 1941. GCI guidance enabled controllers to 'talk' a night fighter into contact with enemy bombers over land – something previously impossible. GCI was still in the early stages of development – one drawback was that the controller could only guide one fighter at a time. The system eventually revolutionized the previously haphazard nature of night fighting.

The most significant result of the vast amount of fire damage in Manchester and in the 'Second Great Fire of London' was Herbert Morrison's national 'fire-watcher' scheme (later known as the 'Fire Guard'). Their job was to report the location of fallen incendiaries and, if safe to do so, render them harmless. The fire-watchers undoubtedly saved hundreds of buildings and millions of pounds of damage. The full impact of the Blitz around Britain in late 1940 was demonstrated by the passing of the National Service Act the following April. The Act, which gave the government the right to conscript men for the Civil Defence Service, confirmed Civil Defence as the country's fourth Service.

The Battle of the Ports (19 February–10 May 1941)

On 6 February 1941, Hitler issued Führer Directive No 23: 'Directions for operations against the English war economy'. In a review of the campaign to January 1941, Hitler noted that, 'the heaviest effect of our operations against the English war economy has lain in the high losses of merchant shipping … increased by the destruction of port installations'. The directive admitted, 'The effect of direct air attacks against the English armaments industry is difficult to estimate', but went on, 'the destruction of many factories and the consequent disorganization of the armaments industry must lead to a considerable fall in production'. Hitler conceded that, 'The least effect of all (as far as we can see) has been made upon the morale and will to resist of the English people'.

The rest of the directive went on to outline the three objectives for the bombing campaign during the spring of 1941:

1. To intensify the *Handelskrieg* against Britain. The directive also noted that, 'we are unable to maintain the scope of our air attacks, as the demands of other theatres of war compel us to withdraw increasingly large air forces from operations against the British Isles'.
2. To prevent British reinforcement in the Mediterranean, Balkan and North African theatres: 'By reducing the available enemy tonnage not only will the blockade, which is decisive to the war, be intensified, but enemy operations in Europe or Africa will be impeded.'
3. To distract attention from preparations for Operation *Barbarossa*: 'Until the beginning of the regrouping of forces for "Barbarossa", efforts will be made to intensify the effect of air and sea warfare … in order to give the impression that an attack on the British Isles is planned for this year.'

The Swansea and Cardiff Blitzes

Swansea was attacked on 17/18 January, when 88 aircraft of Luftflotte 3 bombed the town centre and docks. Poor weather precluded further large-scale Luftwaffe operations until 19 February. That evening, the improving weather over the west of the British Isles and the easily recognizable outline of Swansea Bay, encouraged Luftflotte 3 to make the first of three consecutive attacks on the small port. None of the attacks were opened by the specialist target-markers and this, in combination with a waning moon, may have contributed to an average of only 61 aircraft (82 per cent of aircraft dispatched) claiming to have attacked Swansea. The bombing made 2,000 homeless and seriously disrupted the port's railway

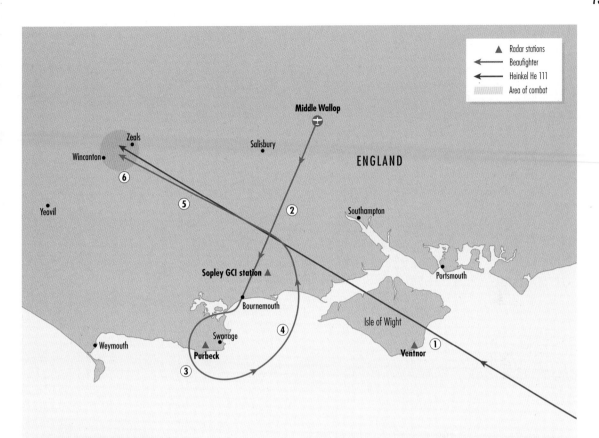

Radar stations
Beaufighter
Heinkel He 111
Area of combat

Middle Wallop

Zeals

Wincanton

Yeovil

⑥

⑤

Salisbury

ENGLAND

②

Southampton

Sopley GCI station ▲

Bournemouth

Portsmouth

④

Isle of Wight

Swanage

Purbeck

Weymouth

③

Ventnor

①

English Channel

Map points and associated commentary:

1. An inbound raid is detected by the long-range, low-precision Chain Home radar network.

2. After taking-off from Middle Wallop, the night-fighter pilot is guided to a patrol line by the Sector Controller.

3. When needed, the night fighter is passed to the GCI Controller, who takes over the guidance of the night fighter using medium-range, medium-precision radar. The Sector Controller ensures that the night fighter is 'fed' efficiently to the GCI Controller.

4. The GCI Controller guides the night fighter into position. To simplify interceptions, the night fighters use constant-radius turns when given new vectors by the controller.

5. When the enemy bomber is judged to be at extreme AI range (short-range, high-precision radar), the controller orders the fighter's observer to 'flash weapon', the coded command to turn on the aircraft's AI radar. If AI contact is made, the GCI Controller leaves the night fighter crew to complete the interception. If more enemy bombers are present, the GCI Controller requests the next waiting fighter from the Sector Controller and begins another interception.

6. The night fighter's observer uses his AI set to guide his pilot towards the enemy bomber, ideally to a position underneath and slightly behind. The pilot makes visual contact and verifies it is an enemy aircraft. Once satisfied, he calls 'Tally Ho' and engages the bomber. When the interception is finished, the pilot calls the Sector Controller and either returns to base or flies back to the patrol line in readiness for the next interception of the night.

This diagram is based on a real interception made by Sqn Ldr John Cunningham and Sgt 'Jimmy' Rawnsley in a 604 Sqn Beaufighter on the night of 13/14 April 1941. The combat resulted in an unverified claim for a Heinkel He 111 'destroyed'.

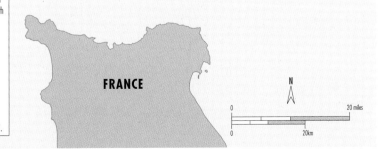

FRANCE

N

0   20 miles
0   20km

services. Some 'trekking' (the term used when a town's inhabitants left to seek refuge in the countryside and surrounding villages) was observed but Home Security thought the population was not disheartened. The port itself escaped largely unscathed.

The heaviest attacks on Cardiff took place on 3/4 and 4/5 March by small numbers of aircraft from Luftflotte 3, led by KGr 100. The first attack was blunted when only 47 aircraft from 68 dispatched found the target, while the second was marred by worsening visibility and the lure of a Starfish site, which drew some bombs. Both raids caused only minor damage and the Luftwaffe did not visit either port in strength again for the rest of the Blitz.

The Clydebank Blitz

Clydebank's importance as an industrial area and port is well known. Key points were the Singer sewing machine factory (producing armaments by 1941), the Royal Navy oil depot at Dalnottar and the vast number of shipyards lining the river. The fall of France forced a massive diversion of shipping to the west coast ports. This increase caused serious congestion in the Clyde in particular. Although extensive re-organization had worked wonders over the winter of 1940–41, Clydebank remained ill-prepared for the coming onslaught.

Two heavy attacks were made when the moon was at its fullest and visibility was reportedly excellent. The assault by 236 aircraft on 13/14 March struck west and north-west Glasgow, and severely damaged the docks and yards at Clydebank. The follow-up attack on 14/15 March by 203 bombers hit the residential area of Clydebank, where casualties were made worse by the collapse of three tenement blocks.

A Heinkel He 111 crew receives a last-minute briefing for the camera, dated March 1941. The kapok lifejackets are gone, replaced by less bulky inflatable versions. Crews found themselves flying more in spring 1941 as units were withdrawn for re-equipment in Germany or deployed to the Balkans. (ullstein bild Dtl./ Contributor, Getty)

Aircrew reports and intelligence assessments were optimistic, some crews declaring the attacks were the most devastating they had yet witnessed. The Singer factory and the naval oil depot were very badly damaged. The raids destroyed 4,300 out of a total of 12,000 homes, killing 1,200 people and seriously injuring another 1,000. However, damage to the docks was not severe and, by April 1941, Clydeside was the only west coast port showing an increase in shipping arrivals since the summer of the previous year.

Problems over Bristol

A major effort by Luftflotte 3 on 16/17 March against Bristol and Avonmouth went badly awry. The operation was compromised from the outset by cloud, which forced most of the attackers to bomb by dead reckoning. Between 2030 and 2100 hours, the first wave of 76 aircraft, led by III/KG 26, began bombing south-west Bristol. At 2130, 80 Wing ordered the Starfish site at Downside, some six miles due south of Avonmouth, to be lit. The site failed to draw any bombs and by 2330 the raid on Bristol had finished. Energetic firefighting had extinguished all the fires in Bristol by 0200, when a second wave of 108 bombers arrived, searching for the docks at Avonmouth. In the murky weather, crews 'plastered' the still-burning Downside site with bombs. The raid vindicated the Starfish programme and demonstrated that poor visibility, efficient firefighting and a well-sited decoy site could work together against an attacking force.

Hull, Plymouth-Devonport

The first major attack on the port of Hull was made on 18/19 March, when a large number of new and inexperienced crews were sent to gain experience over a target considered to be relatively easy to find. Although the attack, led by KGr 100, was made in good visibility, the bombing lacked concentration and even spread to the seaside resort of Scarborough. Around 40 of the 419 aircraft dispatched to Hull chose alternative targets, including London.

Two raids made against the important naval base at Plymouth-Devonport on 20/21 and 21/22 March were more successful. The first attack, short, sharp and benefiting from good visibility, was well-concentrated on the Devonport and Sutton Pool areas. Luftwaffe crews on the second raid reportedly used the positions of Starfish fires noted on the previous night to plot their course to Plymouth. That attack damaged the water mains, and the town centre was almost completely destroyed by fire. The Home Security report was candid: 'All buildings within an area of a quarter of a mile east and west of the Guildhall, and 300 yards north and south of it are completely demolished… Some 5,000 people were rendered homeless and about 6,500 houses damaged.' Meanwhile, the naval dockyard and the key point factories in the area 'escaped lightly'.

London

The capital retained its place in the OKL target list. London was attacked on 8/9 March, at the beginning of the month's first quarter of the lunar phase. The night is chiefly remembered for two SC 50 bombs which penetrated into the underground Café de Paris, hitherto advertised as the safest nightclub in London. One bomb failed to explode but the other killed 34 people, including Ken Johnson, the venue's well-known bandleader.

More incendiaries were dropped on London on 19/20 March than on any previous raid. Crews arriving later found the target area – the dock area between London Bridge and the Thames loop – obscured by vast clouds of smoke. Fires joined together to produce three giant conflagrations in the Port of London and at one point there were so many fires (1,881

A Clydebank soup kitchen. The raids on Clydebank on 13/14 and 14/15 March destroyed 4,300 homes. As predicted, the worker was now in the front-line. Without the development of various lines of support, including programmes for feeding, salvage, repair and rehousing, productivity would have suffered far more than it did. (Print Collector/ Contributor, Getty)

This photograph, dated 18 March 1941, shows an incident in Bristol which may have occurred on the night the Starfish decoy at Downside was so successful. One can only guess the surprise presumably felt by the car's driver. (Daily Herald Archive/Contributor, Getty)

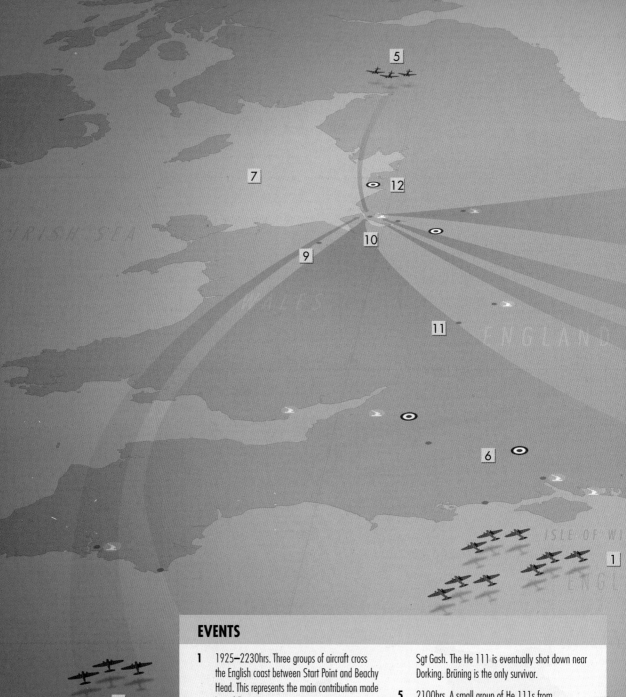

EVENTS

1 1925–2230hrs. Three groups of aircraft cross the English coast between Start Point and Beachy Head. This represents the main contribution made by Luftflotte 3.

2 1930–0300hrs. Bombers from Luftflotte 2 begin to cross the east coast from Holland and Denmark. A smaller raid comes in over East Kent from the Calais area.

3 2020–0300hrs. Another stream of Luftflotte 2 aircraft makes landfall between the Thames Estuary and south-east Anglia.

4 2055hrs. The 5./KG 55 He 111 of Stabsfeldwebel Karl Brüning is intercepted near Beachy Head. The assailant is a 264 Sqn Defiant, crewed by the successful partnership of Flying Officer Hughes and

Sgt Gash. The He 111 is eventually shot down near Dorking. Brüning is the only survivor.

5 2100hrs. A small group of He 111s from KG 26 fly from Stavanger to the Merseyside area. These aircraft probably lay mines off Anglesey and in Liverpool Bay. For various reasons, other bombers attack targets across Britain, including Southampton, Portsmouth, Plymouth, Cardiff and Swansea, as well as a number of British airfields.

6 2121hrs. At about the time that Brüning's He 111 is crashing to earth, Fw Jakob Herrmann's 6./KG 76 Ju 88, flying north, is spotted by Flying Officer Geddes of 604 Sqn. The Beaufighter closes in and, after a devastating burst of fire, the Junkers hits the ground near Warminster. Only one crew member parachutes to safety.

The defences fight back, Liverpool, 12/13 March 1941

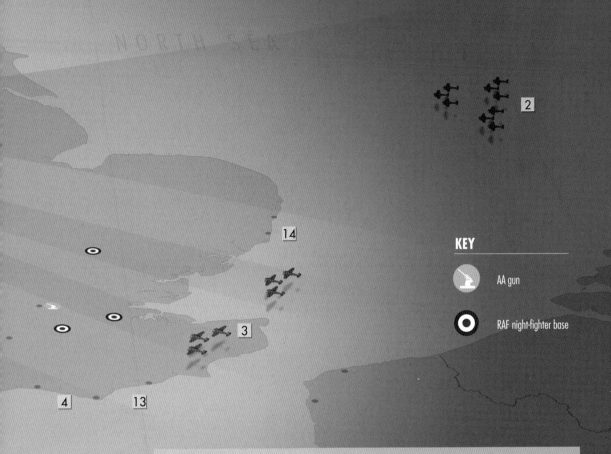

KEY

⚓ AA gun

◎ RAF night-fighter base

EVENTS

7 2124hrs. Shortly after releasing its bombs over Liverpool, Fw Günther Unger's 9./KG 76 Ju 88 is hit by AA fire. Unger orders his crew to bale out. After setting the autopilot to take the Ju 88 out over the Irish Sea, he too takes to his parachute.

8 2130–2350hrs. Another bomber stream, probably composed of aircraft from I and II/KG 27, crosses the coast between Plymouth and Start Point.

9 2155hrs. Unger's abandoned Ju 88 makes a wide circle over the Irish Sea and crosses the north Wales coast. It is intercepted and further damaged over Ruthin by a 307 Sqn Defiant flying from Squires Gate.

10 2210hrs. Oberfeldwebel Karl Singler's He 111 of 6./KG 55 turns for home over the target and is attacked by a 96 Sqn Hurricane flown by Sgt McNair. The bomber hits a balloon cable and crashes near Widnes, leaving three survivors.

11 2255hrs. An hour and a half after it was abandoned by its crew over Liverpool, Unger's Ju

88 is fired on by an AA battery near Birmingham, before it finally crashes near Wychbold.

12 2310hrs. A 96 Sqn Defiant, flown by Flying Officer Vesely and Sgt Haycock, engages a German bomber over Liverpool. Haycock's guns jam and Vesely is wounded by return fire. The combat is broken off.

13 2345hrs. A 4./KG 27 Junkers Ju 88, fleeing south-eastwards, is caught by a 264 Sqn Defiant. The Junkers is shot down, crashing into the sea some 15 miles off Hastings.

14 0150hrs. Pilot Officer Stevens intercepts a Junkers Ju 88 near Orford Ness. The bomber is damaged but Stevens is forced to abandon the pursuit when some 25 miles out to sea. The Ju 88 may have been Leutnant Arno Kick's aircraft from II/KG 30, which force-landed at Gilze-Rijen with its pilot wounded.

15 Two more He 111s ditch off the French coast and their crews are rescued. A third Heinkel is lost without trace.

The fashionable Café de Paris nightclub was hit on the night of 8/9 March, killing 34 people. Sir Malcolm Sargent considered the scherzo of Vaughan Williams's Sixth Symphony to be a musical depiction of the incident – although this was denied by the composer. (Daily Herald Archive/Contributor, Getty)

were officially recorded) that the bomber crews were unable to count them all. Casualties were at an all-time high: 631 people were killed, 150 of which were in West Ham.

The anti-shipping campaign

The Luftwaffe's attacks on the ports were complemented by a maritime campaign (see Table 4). However, the Luftwaffe's anti-shipping forces found themselves part of a power struggle between the Kriegsmarine on the one hand and Göring on the other.

The specialist minelaying units were small, few in number and as such were unable to adequately cover the myriad harbours and estuaries around the British Isles. The success or otherwise of the Luftwaffe's minelaying is hard to quantify but the relatively small number of vessels lost to mines in this period underlines the unfulfilled potential of the campaign.

The attacks on ships themselves, either at sea or near the coast, were more successful. From August, the Condors of KG 40 made armed-reconnaissance patrols between Bordeaux-Mérignac and Aalborg, up to 370 miles (600km) west of Britain. KG 40 was unable to make any more than two sorties a day, which was simply not enough to assist Dönitz's U-boat campaign. One notable success came on 26 October 1940, when the 42,000-ton Canadian Pacific liner *Empress of Britain* was badly damaged off the north-west coast of Ireland by a Condor and sunk by a U-boat two days later. Attacks on ships in harbour, seemingly easy targets, proved otherwise: only 20 vessels were sunk in harbour in the 12 months from July 1940. Improved British defences, which included coastal fighter patrols and increased AA defences on merchantmen and escort vessels, forced the anti-shipping Kampfgruppen to resort to dawn and dusk attacks around the coasts.

Large-scale activity only resumed in the spring of 1941. Between February and May, there were 776 anti-shipping sorties and 875 minelaying sorties. Unfortunately, the hope that a new Luftwaffe-controlled Atlantic command, *FliegerFührer Atlantik*, would work with the

'A giant goes into the deep' crowed Nazi propaganda, after the *Empress of Britain* was crippled by Bernhard Jope's Condor, then sunk by a U-boat off the coast of Ireland in October 1940. The liner was KG 40's biggest 'scalp'. The Condor's crew pose for the photographer. (Mondadori Portfolio/Contributor, Getty)

A Condor of KG 40 attacking a convoy in the North Atlantic, May 1941. The spring Blitz was intended to work with the war at sea. Despite their fearsome reputation, the small number of Condors meant that their support of Dönitz's U-boats was not as effective as it could have been. (Mirrorpix/ Contributor, Getty)

U-boats in reporting and attacking British convoys never really came to anything. KG 40 was prone to communicating inaccurate convoy positions, while the U-boats frequently failed to receive the messages sent to them. Overall, there was little coordination between the two services and Luftwaffe support for the U-boats was more incidental than concerted.

Crescendo: 7 April–10 May

Poor weather and the darker nights of the new moon period halted major Luftwaffe operations in late March and early April. Operations in the Balkans meant the withdrawal of several Kampfgruppen, while I/KG 1, redesignated III/KG 40, transferred to Brest in the anti-shipping role. Other units returned from rest and re-equipment with the Ju 88.

The later weeks of the Luftwaffe's campaign in April and May 1941 were distinguished by five main 'Blitzes' on Greenock, Belfast, Plymouth, Merseyside and London. The Luftwaffe also returned to the Midlands with raids on Birmingham, Coventry and a disastrous foray against Derby.

The Greenock Blitz

On 7/8 April, early in the first lunar quarter, a large raid was made against Greenock, Dumbarton and Hillington. Despite good visibility, a large proportion of aircraft failed to reach the Glasgow area (of 213 Luftflotte 3 aircraft dispatched to Clydeside, only 97 claimed to have reached the target). Fifty-two aircraft were assigned to the Rolls-Royce Merlin engine works at Hillington. Two more raids, concentrating on Greenock, Paisley and Dumbarton, came on 5/6 and 6/7 May. Both attacks fell mainly on the residential areas of these towns, where they caused massive damage and, according to official estimates, killed 306 people.

Loss of life in the shelters and houses near to the docks and shipyards was disproportionately heavy. Yet the Kampfgeschwader were hampered by distance, frequently poor weather and relatively light bombloads. They do not appear to have come near to stopping, or even much reducing, the flow of imports into the Clyde, and this trio of attacks were the last major raids on Clydeside.

Failure over Portsmouth

The last major attack on Portsmouth was made on 17/18 April. The raid was opened by Luftflotte 2, followed by a second wave from Luftflotte 3. None of the latter's pathfinder units participated, which may partly account for the raid's failure. The Starfish on Hayling Island, only three miles from the town centre, was ignited quickly as the first bombers

'Plymouth as a business and commercial centre', wrote a Home Security report, 'has ceased to exist.' These citizens of the naval port put on a brave face for the camera in 1941. (Keystone/Stringer, Getty)

arrived over Portsmouth. The misty weather proved ideal in 'selling the ruse' and the diffused light from the Starfish quickly began to attract bombs. Early in the raid, an intercepted German radio message reported that although mist obscured Portsmouth, fires could be observed. From that point, only two aircraft appear to have found the real target – the rest of the 144 aircraft bombed the decoy and nearby mudflats with 170 high explosive bombs, 32 parachute mines and 5,000 incendiaries.

The Belfast Blitz

Together with the Clyde, Belfast was the most remote of the Luftwaffe's major targets. The port, which was home to the large Harland & Wolff shipyards and the Short & Harland aircraft factory, was attacked four times in April and May 1941.

Just 180 (55 per cent) of the 327 aircraft dispatched to Belfast on 15/16 April claimed to bomb the target. Most of those that failed to reach Belfast were diverted due to poor weather, with 51 making for Merseyside instead. Belfast was divided into three concentration points: the first and second covered the north-west and eastern dock areas, the latter dominated by Harland & Wolff and Short & Harland. The third aiming-point was the town centre. Aside from the aircraft which diverted to Liverpool, Luftflotte 2 made a smaller raid on Tyneside and Luftflotte 3 attacked Portland. The raid made around 20,000 people homeless and some fires were still burning by nightfall on the following day.

The second major raid on Belfast came on 4/5 May, in the midst of the 'Merseyside Blitz'. Of the 270 aircraft dispatched by Luftflotte 3, only 167 (62 per cent) reached the target. The *Schwerpunkt* was the docks and shipyards, but the town suffered most. A smaller follow-up attack was delivered on 5/6 May.

The city's remoteness from Europe and wrangling between Westminster and the Northern Irish government over who should pay for the Civil Defences had left Belfast badly unprepared. There were fewer air raid shelter spaces per head than anywhere else and civilian casualties were proportionally high. The Easter Tuesday raid may have killed 900 and injured another 1,500, making it the most lethal on any city outside London.

The Plymouth-Devonport Blitz

Plymouth-Devonport suffered three consecutive raids on the nights of 21/22, 22/23 and 23/24 April. The first left 30 large fires and caused heavy casualties in the town centre. The most effective raid of the trio came on the second night. Telephone communications were put out of action and the town's control centre had to be evacuated. Firefighting was hindered and a high wind fanned the flames across the town. The situation was so bad that some fires were still burning the following evening, when they acted as a guide for the third raid.

The fourth attack, on 28/29 April, caused some damage to the dockyard but little to the town. The last raid, made the following night, began badly, when wood fires at Mount Edgcumbe to the south of Devonport attracted the attention of most of the first wave. Later bombing by the second wave was more accurate, and a gasholder and the Tor Point oil storage depot were set alight. The commercial and residential centre was devastated, increasing pressure on the town's everyday needs in food and utilities.

Plymouth had been dealt with savagely. Around 40,000 people were left homeless after the five raids, with nearly 600 killed and 450 seriously injured. While a Cabinet report noted that, 'Plymouth has rallied with vigour from all attacks', a later Home Intelligence assessment was unequivocal. 'For the present,' it read, 'Plymouth as a business and commercial centre of a prosperous countryside has ceased to exist.' The same memorandum mentioned trekking and 'evidence of a good deal of defeatist talk' but conceded that the 'morale of the people as a whole appeared to be good'.

Disaster over Derby

The intention for the night of 8/9 May was to attack Sheffield in strength, while smaller raids were made against Derby and Nottingham. However, considerable cloud cover in the Midlands and north obscured the targets, and the attacks went badly awry. Much of the force intended for Sheffield instead diverted to Hull, which received the brunt of the night's bombing.

Meanwhile, the Heinkels of KGr 100, originally detailed to mark the Rolls-Royce works at Derby, found their target obscured and they eventually flew north-east to assist the assault on Hull. In an effort to divert the attack on Derby, 80 Wing ordered a Starfish site to be lit at Cropwell Butler, to the east of Nottingham. Derby was little damaged and by the time the second force of bombers arrived in search of Nottingham, the Starfish was well alight. This may have been the cause of confusion among the bomber crews, who appeared to assume the Starfish to be Derby burning from the earlier attack and used the fire as a guide for their own bomb run. Some 230 high explosive bombs, together with hundreds of incendiaries, were found to have fallen, more or less harmlessly, well to the east of Nottingham in the Vale of Belvoir.

The Mersey Blitz

The Blitz on Merseyside may have been the most damaging series of raids of the entire campaign. The Liverpool-Birkenhead area was targeted on 26/27 April and then every night over the first week of May. The first attack was marred by cloud cover: only 92 crews from both Luftflotten found the target and scattered bombing resulted. The heaviest raids came on 2/3, 3/4 and 7/8 May. The attack on 3/4 May was the most destructive. Visibility was good: no specialist marking was needed and the attacking crews had no difficulty in finding their target areas on the east bank of the Mersey. The fires which broke out were officially described, with some understatement, as 'serious'. Emergency aid from outside the Liverpool area was badly hindered by widespread damage to telephone lines.

Several ships were sunk in the port. One, the SS *Malakand*, loaded with around 1,000 tons of munitions destined for the Middle East, was berthed in the Huskisson No 2 Dock. As the raid progressed, flames from a nearby warehouse spread to the ship and eventually, in desperation, the ship was scuttled. A few hours after the all clear sounded, the *Malakand* exploded, destroying the

Liverpool after seven consecutive attacks, May 1941. Although activity at the docks was scarcely affected, Whitehall worried that destruction on this scale would become unbearable for the city's population. A few days later, the Blitz was over. (Mirrorpix/Contributor, Getty)

Sir Christopher Wren's St Clement Danes, gutted by fire on the night of 10/11 May 1941, was one of many post-Great Fire churches damaged or destroyed in the Blitz. It was rebuilt and re-consecrated as the Central Church of the Royal Air Force in 1958. (Print Collector/Contributor, Getty)

dock. Plates from the ship were found 2½ miles away but, incredibly, only four civilians died in the explosion. It was 74 hours before the fires burned themselves out.

The final attack, on 7/8 May, caused massive damage and a good deal of alarm in Whitehall. Visibility over Merseyside was initially poor and a number of bombers were diverted to Hull before the cloud cover dispersed. The Bootle district was badly damaged: 4,000–5,000 houses were destroyed, another 14,000 damaged and 20,000 people made homeless. Some fires were reported to be still burning on 10 May. Heavy damage to roads and railways brought all movement in and out of the docks to a stop.

For a period, the percentage of goods landed was estimated at only 25 per cent of the usual total. The Mersey Blitz rendered 118 out of 130 deep-draught berths temporarily unusable, killed 3,966 people and seriously injured 3,812. A staggering 70,000 civilians were made homeless. A Home Intelligence report made some weeks later came to the conclusion that, 'Liverpool has a depressed and sordid atmosphere' (which was perhaps unsurprising given the circumstances), adding that, 'morale in general seems good', although, 'a strong undercurrent of anxiety' existed.

London

The largest raid of the Blitz to date was made against London on 16/17 April. The concentration point was the dock area extending from Tower Bridge, and the density of flames and smoke made bomb-aiming difficult. Some crews made two or even three sorties, and one of the last to depart the target area reported 80 major conflagrations and so many smaller fires they could not be counted. Luftwaffe Intelligence considered the attack to be the most effective since the beginning of the campaign. The bombing spread over 66 boroughs and started 2,251 fires, eight of which were major and 41 serious. There was large-scale damage in central London but the dock area was only slightly damaged. One of the more famous victims of the Blitz – the bandleader Al Bowlly – was killed on this night in his flat in St James, not, as is sometimes believed, in the Café de Paris disaster of 8/9 March.

Only three nights later, the Luftwaffe launched the famous 'Thousand-ton raid', when 1,026 tons of high explosive and 4,252 containers of incendiaries were dropped in the space of seven hours. German propaganda claimed the massive attack was in part revenge for an RAF attack on Berlin and part to celebrate the 52nd birthday of Adolf Hitler. The bomb-aiming was spoilt by a layer of cloud, which only cleared late in the raid. Luftwaffe crews observed enormous fires in the Royal Victoria, East and West India Docks, the grain stores in the Millwall Docks and in Greenwich. Altogether, the bombing spread over a vast area and started 1,460 fires. Over 1,200 people were killed, making the attack not just the heaviest of the entire war but also the deadliest.

London suffered the last major raid of the Blitz – and one of the most damaging – on 10/11 May. Bombers from Luftflotten 2 and 3 made a total of 571 sorties in clear visibility. The bombing inevitably spread across central London and damaged many famous buildings, including Westminster Abbey, the Tower of London and the British Museum. The Wren-designed church of St Clement Danes was gutted by fire.

The defences fight back

For the RAF, by early March, there were signs that the Luftwaffe were preparing a series of attacks on the west coast ports. Sholto Douglas accordingly strengthened the fighter cover of the Merseyside area, while 185 heavy anti-aircraft guns were redistributed to the west coast, although this created shortages elsewhere. Another redisposition came with the shorter spring nights in April, when an increase in the night-fighter defence of the southern ports became necessary.

Operation *Fighter Night*

Sholto Douglas had been an advocate of the 'cat's eyes' or non-AI fighters from the beginning. The perennial problem of locating and intercepting raiders in darkness still remained, however. A solution was Operation *Fighter Night* or the 'layer patrol'. Single-seaters patrolled in altitude layers on clear nights, when the moon was above the horizon, either on the approaches to a target, where they might be able to fly inside the *Krokodil*, or over the target where the bombers could be illuminated by the area's searchlights. AA batteries in the area were ordered to confine their shooting to 2,000ft below the lowest fighter layer, or to withhold fire completely. The only disadvantage of the *Fighter Night* was the disgruntlement of the town's population when the AA guns failed to fire their usual barrage.

Seventeen *Fighter Nights* were flown during the Blitz, the first over Portsmouth on 10/11 January. Early results were somewhat indifferent. A *Fighter Night* was flown by 87 Sqn over Bristol on 16 January during which 'nothing was seen at all except fires on the ground and bombs bursting'. Matters improved with the clearer nights during the spring. The non-AI fighters enjoyed their most successful night on 10/11 May, claiming 12 bombers when a concentration of targets in a small area and in clear moonlight provided ideal conditions. A similar concept was used with success later in the war by the Luftwaffe, when it instituted the *Wilde Sau* ('Wild Sow') night-fighter defence. The RAF's *Fighter Nights*, though valuable in the spring of 1941, did not represent the future of night air defence over Britain, and Table 1 in the 'Aftermath and Analysis' chapter illustrates the superiority of the GCI/AI fighter system.

The turning point arrived with the improved weather during the attacks on Liverpool and Clydeside on 12/13 and 13/14 March. No 96 Sqn, based at Squires Gate near Blackpool, were overjoyed:

'At last!' was the spoken comment… It was difficult to believe that after such a rotten weather period that one could have patrols of 6 aircraft … and that the jerries would come along at the same time. It seemed too good to be true… No finer tonic was ever ladled out to a night-fighter squadron … one could see everywhere unmistakeable signs that there would be trouble one day for the Heinkels and Junkers that poke their noses near our patrol area.

GCI, which had promised success for so long, finally delivered in March, April and May. On 13 March, AI Beaufighters claimed

Flt Sgt Edward Thorn (left) and Sgt Frederick Barker were the most successful Defiant partnership of the war, claiming 11 aircraft during the Battle of Britain. Their 12th came on the night of 9/10 April 1941, when they shot down a 5./KG 55 Heinkel He 111 near Godalming. (IWM CH 2526 (AHB))

An Air Ministry Experimental Station Type 15 mobile GCI station: the first version of GCI radar. The mobile stations could be set up or dismantled in just hours. The first batch of six stations had a number of limitations, including poor height-finding. Later versions were much improved. (CH 15198 (AHB))

nine aircraft destroyed and two probables. From this point onward, the claims – if not certified kills – rose steadily. This increase in success can be attributed to four main factors:

1. By February, there were four squadrons either equipped, or in the process of re-equipping, with Beaufighters. In addition, more GCI stations were opening each month: six in January, one in March, four in April and two in May.
2. The increase in frequency and size of Luftwaffe attacks, which (as with the non-AI fighters) provided the GCI/AI night fighters with more targets.
3. The lighter and clearer spring nights, which gave both types of night fighter more opportunities to make visual interceptions.
4. Increasing familiarity at the GCI stations and on the squadrons with the radar equipment, together with a consequent improvement in the teamwork between the GCI controllers and the AI pilots and observers.

Sholto Douglas put these successes in context in his Dispatch: 'The cumulative effect', he wrote, 'of the ever-increasing losses which the Germans incurred as the defences got under way … were not sufficient in themselves to have brought the offensive to a standstill.' The overall loss rate in the Kampfgeschwader, even in the last months of the Blitz, was only 159 from all causes, from 4,442 sorties. Sholto Douglas then added, 'We were confident … that if the enemy had not chosen that moment to pull out, we should have soon been inflicting such casualties that the continuance of his night offensive on a similar scale would have been impossible.'

AA Command

AA Command battled not only the enemy but an insufficiency of guns and poorly trained crews throughout the campaign. By the end of the Blitz, there were only 1,691 guns in AA Command, against the pre-war approved scale of 2,232. The 3.7in. gun was not produced in the numbers required, partly due to the effects of enemy bombing on towns such as Birmingham and Sheffield.

One way to make up for the shortage of guns was the Unrotated Projectile or Z Battery. The batteries came in a variety of forms but all fired a 3in. solid fuel rocket, similar to that later used by the RAF for ground attack missions. The surface-to-air version was fitted with a high explosive warhead detonated by a time fuse. Churchill and Lindemann were ardent supporters but actual service use proved extremely disappointing. Accuracy was poor (the rocket projectiles flew in all directions), and reloading 128 rockets proved laborious in the extreme. Production delays and priority for Admiralty orders meant that only a few Z Batteries saw service during the Blitz.

AA Command's success-rate worsened from February (2,963 rounds fired per aircraft destroyed) to March (5,870 rounds per aircraft). In April, the figure improved again, to 3,165 rounds per aircraft, but in May deteriorated to 4,610 rounds. This variable performance can be attributed to the Fighter Nights – which restricted AA fire – and the dispersion of Luftwaffe attacks across multiple targets, which frustrated concentration of gun batteries. If AA Command's claims were somewhat optimistic, it is likely that their fire, in the words of Sholto Douglas, 'prevented leisurely and methodical bombing from low altitudes'. This was certainly the experience of Bomber Command when faced with intense German flak during the same period.

With the exception of Clydeside and Belfast, all the targets which received major raids during the final phase of the Blitz had already been attacked in strength earlier in the campaign. The Civil Defences were therefore reasonably prepared for what was to come. The intensity of some of the attacks did test some areas to their limit, in particular Plymouth-Devonport and Merseyside. At these and other towns, support for those trekking and the subsequent recovery efforts by official and voluntary organizations went a long way to relieve the situation. That more damage was not sustained is a tribute to the fire-watchers and the fire services. One legacy of the Blitz was the decision to combine the local authority fire brigades and AFS to form the National Fire Service in August 1941.

Although the inhabitants of London and elsewhere did not know, the attacks on the capital on 10/11 May and Birmingham on 16/17 May were the last raids of the Blitz. The Luftwaffe had already begun a redeployment eastward during April and by June only 16 Kampfgruppen, most of which were primarily anti-shipping units, were left. The Luftwaffe had brought down the curtain on the first strategic bombing campaign of World War II.

John Cunningham and observer 'Jimmy' Rawnsley were the most successful night-fighter team during the Blitz. They claimed 11 victories between February and the end of May 1941, including three on the night of 15/16 April. Cunningham went on to a distinguished post-war career as a test pilot for de Havilland. (IWM CH 12224 (AHB))

John Cunningham's most successful night

In the early hours of 16 April 1941, Heinkel He 111P-2, G1+ES of 8./KG 55, was returning homewards. The crew were unaware that they were being tracked by a Beaufighter flown by Sqn Ldr John Cunningham and Sgt 'Jimmy' Rawnsley. Cunningham had already spotted anti-aircraft fire near Marlborough, before Rawnsley's AI set detected the Heinkel as it passed in front of the Beaufighter. Cunningham turned after the Heinkel and, after identifying the aircraft against the night sky, pulled up the nose of the Beaufighter and opened fire from a range of 80yds. The attack caught the Heinkel's crew by complete surprise. Cunningham reported a 'big flash' in the fuselage, after which the Heinkel dived away to the left. Fire broke out inside the aircraft. The pilot, Oberleutnant Günther von Siedlitz, jettisoned the bombs, then ordered the crew to abandon the stricken aircraft. Two of the crew, Unteroffiziers H. Sauer and H. Rosenberg, escaped, although one, already wounded, broke his leg on landing. The aircraft's Beobachter, Feldwebel F. Hümmer, was killed when his parachute was apparently torn off when it struck a balloon cable. Siedlitz's parachute failed to open properly and he too was killed. The wreckage of the Heinkel crashed into an abandoned house in Padwell Road, Portswood, where it burned itself out. This was Cunningham's second of three claims on 15/16 April.

AFTERMATH AND ANALYSIS

The aftermath of the Blitz

The bombing killed 42,629 civilians and seriously injured another 50,000 between August 1940 and May 1941. This represented over half the total British civilian casualties in World War II. Until autumn 1942, more civilians had been killed than British soldiers. It is estimated that in London alone, one in six people were made homeless at some point. For the Luftwaffe, the campaign was a cheap one: a mere 518 German bombers were lost from all causes between October 1940 and May 1941. Yet Germany's aims went unfulfilled. Why?

The Blitz began with day and night attacks on Liverpool and then London – the consequence of the search for a quick decision in the Battle of Britain. The night offensive on the capital continued for over two months and the supposed aims – to render the Port of London useless and bring civilian morale to breaking point – went unrealized. The volume of trade passing through the east and south coast ports had already begun to decline before the Blitz began. 'At no time', stated a Home Security memorandum, 'have the docks and their outer basins been rendered unserviceable'.

When the failure of the Blitz on London became obvious, the campaign moved nationwide with the offensive against the inland towns and ports. The most notable success was against Coventry, where bright moonlight, the concentration of factories in a small area, narrow medieval streets and a small, overwhelmed fire service combined to produce a perfect storm of circumstances. The major attack on Sheffield a month later likewise utilized the full moon, and the large attacking force was able to deluge the small target. Raids on Birmingham and Manchester, hampered by scattered bombing, were less fruitful.

Attacks on the steel industry were relatively few and according to Home Security, output remained 'satisfactory'. Overall, loss of production in 1941 due to air raids was 208,924 tons of pig iron and 246,708 tons of finished steel. Of the latter, 237,678 tons, or 95 per cent, was due to production stoppages caused by air raid warnings. In other words, the bombing served to dislocate production more effectively than it destroyed plant or materiel. These losses must be put into perspective: in 1941, 7,393,000 tons of pig iron and 10,127,000 tons of finished steel were produced. Birmingham suffered only four more major raids after December 1940 and Sheffield none, excluding the abortive attempt on 8/9 May 1941.

In a secret memorandum concerning damage to the aircraft industry, Home Security reported that, 'There has been no case of damage which could be interpreted as a catastrophe to the industry.' The Ministry of Aircraft Production's target, issued in October 1940, of manufacturing over 2,500 aircraft per month by June 1941 was frustrated more by the precautionary dispersal of subcontractors; the effect of industrial dispersal was more serious than bomb damage. British aircraft production remained higher in 1940 and 1941 than German intelligence estimates suggested. Table 2 shows that industrial production as a whole suffered little dislocation.

The main cause of industrial stoppages in 1941 was the damage to utilities. Gas supply losses were considered negligible. The cutting of electricity seemed to be worse in January, when Portsmouth was cut off for two and a half days, Plymouth for one day and Bristol for 16½ hours. The worst affected was Greenock, where in May the supply was interrupted for five days. Losses in oil storage, despite the Luftwaffe's efforts, were tiny: equating to just 0.5 per cent of oil stocks as at the end of December 1941.

Winston Churchill surveys the House of Commons, 11 May 1941. Almost exactly a year earlier, Churchill had given his famous 'blood, toil, tears and sweat' speech in this very place, now a hollow ruin. (Print Collector/ Contributor, Getty)

Attacks on the ports remained the campaign's most consistent theme. Between 14 November 1940 and 7 March 1941, there were 31 major raids. Twenty-five (81 per cent) of these were against ports (including London) and only six on inland towns. On average, there was a raid on a port target every four and a half days.

During the campaign's third phase (8 March–11 May), there were 38 major raids in 63 days, due to improved weather conditions. Thirty-three (87 per cent) of these were against ports (again including London) and only five on inland towns. This averaged one major attack on a port target every two days. Overall, between 14 November 1940 and 10 May 1941, there were 69 major raids, 58 (84 per cent) of which were against ports and 11 on inland towns.

Table 3 shows the reduction in trade via the south and east coast ports, and the resulting burden on the west coast in the winter of 1940–41. This dislocation, which was being addressed by 1941, had a greater effect on overseas trade than the Luftwaffe's bombing in the spring of that year. The strenuous efforts which went into re-organizing the ports in the winter of 1940–41 eventually paid off, for ships were unloaded quickly and, as a rule, the cargoes transported away. Supplies destroyed in storage at the ports were very small in relation to the overall volume of imports. Losses in food due to bombing during 1941 came to 271,500 tons, of which only 70,590 tons could not be recovered and subsequently used. This contrasts to losses of food and feeding stuffs at sea for 1941 of 787,200 tons. Dönitz's U-boats were far more dangerous than Göring's air attacks.

More critical was the railway system, damage to which could impose serious delays in the transport of supplies from the ports to the rest of the country. Despite damage around London and Liverpool, the network suffered few lasting delays and the plethora of railway lines helped to mitigate what could have been a serious supply situation.

The week of heavy attacks on Merseyside and Hull in early May caused heavy and widespread damage. Although the populations of these towns suffered more than the ports themselves, rumours that two or three more heavy raids would be enough to put Liverpool out of action altogether seemed to have been very wide of the mark. Delays to ships, according to a rough Home Security estimate, resulted in the loss of about 12,000 tons of imports. Total imports in 1941 came to almost 31,000,000 tons. Most remarkable is that the rate at

The failure of the Luftwaffe's Blitz is rarely disputed. Yet it is all too easy to overlook the suffering of those who died – and those who survived. (Popperfoto/Contributor, Getty)

which ships were turned round in port actually *increased* in May 1941.

Much of the bombing fell on residential areas. These were rarely the stated objectives but the attacks killed and injured many thousands of key workers, while those who escaped unscathed could find their houses destroyed or uninhabitable. A corresponding rise in absenteeism, industrial stoppages and reduced output naturally followed. Contemporary research revealed that loss of production was often temporary but there were exceptions, such as in Coventry, Birmingham and Liverpool, where output could take weeks or even months to fully recover.

Both sides set much store by the effect of bombing on the vague and intangible concept of morale. In a broad sense, it was found that morale recovered once the initial shock subsided and the Civil Defence and relief organizations improved. Solitary or widely spaced attacks (such as those on Coventry, Birmingham and Belfast) gave the town and its population time to recover. However, heavy and repeated attacks could be devastating. That the Luftwaffe recognized this is demonstrated by the examples of Plymouth, Hull and Merseyside, each of which suffered a series of heavy and closely spaced attacks in April and May 1941.

The experiences of those under the bombs differed widely according to their age, sex, class and location. It is therefore difficult to generalize, but it was the working class which suffered most. This group usually lived in close proximity to the areas attacked and, moreover, had difficulty in mitigating the situation in which they found themselves. As a rule, the middle class had the income to buy food, refurbish damaged homes and could, in some cases, move to the country for the short- or medium-term until the worst was over.

The phenomenon of trekking, which caused considerable anxiety in Whitehall, took place all over the country in the Blitzed towns. It was in fact a completely sensible and pragmatic reaction. There was little point remaining in mortal danger. By moving each night to the countryside, a town's citizens were making sure that they were still around to go to work the next day. The government was slow to respond to trekking, although reception areas providing food, drink and basic amenities were authorized, if somewhat grudgingly, in some areas. Yet despite evidence that there was a definite sense of war-weariness in some towns, the public recognized that there was no realistic alternative.

Analysis: Why did the Blitz fail?

From the outset, there was little framework on which the Luftwaffe could build a strategic bombing campaign. The somewhat loosely worded pre-war doctrine was intended to provide commanders with freedom in planning and executing operations. Few within the Luftwaffe had anticipated an independent strategic bombing campaign. On the other hand, the historiological concentration on Luftwaffe doctrine has overshadowed the more important issue of Germany's relative economic weakness. There were simply too few resources to satisfy the demands of the three Services *and* allow the Luftwaffe a strategic bomber force. As a result, the Kampfwaffe was built around medium bombers of small load-carrying capacity.

Yet the fact remains that OKL stumbled along a road with no settled aim or method. The 12-month campaign chopped and changed as the search for an effective strategy was sought: from the war on British trade, to preparations for a seaborne invasion, followed by a campaign against London, then industry and finally a return to the trade war. This operational uncertainty stemmed not only from ambivalent pre-war thinking and poor intelligence work. Hitler was much more concerned with the planning for Operation *Barbarossa*. Göring's interest can be gauged by his decision to take a period of leave which extended from October to the new year.

As it was, the Luftwaffe divided its attacks among a multiplicity of targets. From November 1940 until April 1941, attacks shifted back and forth with little sense of a firm objective. Commenting on the 14/15 November 1940 raid on Coventry, Home Security reported that, 'Had the enemy continued his attack undoubtedly the results to the aircraft industry would have been very serious.' The raid was perhaps the most

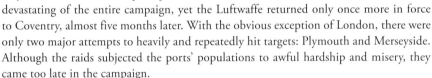

'THIS is London.' The CBS news broadcasts of Ed Murrow from London to the United States during the Blitz became world-famous and undoubtedly played a major role in fuelling American support for Britain. Erik Warr, the Ministry of Information's censor, sits in readiness with the 'kill switch'. (Historical/Contributor, Getty)

devastating of the entire campaign, yet the Luftwaffe returned only once more in force to Coventry, almost five months later. With the obvious exception of London, there were only two major attempts to heavily and repeatedly hit targets: Plymouth and Merseyside. Although the raids subjected the ports' populations to awful hardship and misery, they came too late in the campaign.

Problems at the tactical level bedevilled the campaign. Target-finding, except in the case of London or the south and east coast ports, remained difficult. Target-marking was in its infancy and bombing accuracy often disappointing. The beam systems and high standards of navigation did not confer the advantages expected. Bombload mixes were still at an early stage of development. High explosive continued to form the majority of the loads dropped over Britain but only a small proportion of this was in the form of very heavy bombs and parachute mines. The incendiary, which formed an important part of the later Allied air campaigns, was actually reduced in proportion to high explosive bombs during the later months of the Blitz. Assessing damage was hindered by the limits of post-raid photographic analysis. The Luftwaffe fought the campaign without really knowing how much damage it was inflicting on any one target system – or what the effect of that damage was. Civilian morale meanwhile proved impossible to quantify.

Weather conditions played the single most important part in the entire campaign. Great reliance was placed on attacking during the full moon periods around the middle of each month. The difficulties experienced in the *Mondscheinserenaden* over the industrial Midlands during November and December effectively ruled them out of further operations. The entire campaign was essentially stopped by the winter weather between January and mid-March 1941.

It should be observed that the Luftwaffe possessed a better bomber force than many in 1940–41. RAF Bomber Command, on which so much had been wagered, was frankly incapable of conducting an effective strategic campaign until at least late 1942 or 1943. The Blitz was the first campaign to show that, given a well-organized and well-equipped Civil Defence, a state (encompassing the government, economy and population) could withstand any but the heaviest and most destructive bombing.

These were the immediate aims and consequences of the Blitz. The third phase of the campaign was more successful in the long run. Until *Barbarossa*, air reinforcements from Britain to Greece and North Africa were affected by the perceived need to hold squadrons back for whatever the summer might bring. The whirlwind of attacks which characterized the last weeks of the Blitz may have helped to disguise Hitler's true intentions on Germany's eastern border.

To summarize, the Blitz was hamstrung by political indifference, operational uncertainty and the limitations imposed by the technology of the time. Moreover, it suffered from being the first of its kind: a prototype which revealed some of the wider questions surrounding strategic bombing.

Crucially, the Blitz altered perceptions outside Britain and Germany. This was nowhere more true than in the United States, whose citizens followed the Blitz through the reports of American newspaper correspondents and the radio broadcasts of Ed Murrow. The propaganda film, *London Can Take It*, was cleverly marketed to a primarily American audience. In May 1940, a Gallup poll showed that American public support for sending forces to fight Germany stood at only 7 per cent. By March 1941, support for involvement in the war by helping Britain, even at the risk of the US entering the war, was at 67 per cent.

Historically, the Blitz sits at the junction between the Axis successes of 1939–40 and the turn of the war in 1941–42. The failure to bring Britain to the negotiating table meant Hitler condemned himself to fighting on two fronts, in addition to German commitments in the Mediterranean and North Africa. The expectation of defeating the Soviet Union and returning to deal with Britain never materialized. With the Soviets and then the United States in the war by the end of 1941, the economic and military pressures on the Third Reich would become unsustainable. The Luftwaffe's lack of faith in strategic bombing was confirmed by the Blitz. It would launch bombing campaigns again, notably on the cities of the Soviet Union and in the 'Baedeker' and 'Baby' Blitzes against Britain. British night-fighter defences, honed by the last months of the Blitz, would take a toll on the attackers. None of the Luftwaffe's bombing campaigns, compromised as they were by doctrinal indifference and ebbing strength, would reach the same scale as the Blitz of 1940–41. Although there was little call for retaliatory attacks on Germany, the Blitz provided the grounds for retribution and a mass of evidence on which to base the RAF's own strategic bombing campaign.

Some of the modern buildings which sit among far older ones give today's passers-by a glimpse into the effects of the Blitz around Britain. Of the 14 remaining Blitz ruins, two are the National Picture Theatre in Hull and a portion of the naval dockyard in Portsmouth. The remainder are ecclesiastical. In Coventry, a conscious decision was taken to build alongside – rather than replace – the ruins of the original cathedral. It is no coincidence that Coventry and that other victim of air power – Dresden – have become powerful symbols of post-war reconciliation.

Table 1: Merchant shipping under the British flag: Total losses				
Month	Ships sunk (Total)	Tonnage (Total)	Losses to aircraft (Tonnage)	% Loss to aircraft
August	59	279,100	49,600	18
September	66	324,800	45,100	14
October	68	302,400	4,600	1.5
November	76	313,100	54,000	17
December	63	257,400	7,900	3
January	45	209,600	47,200	23
February	80	316,300	51,900	16
March	98	366,800	70,300	19
April	79	362,500	122,500	34
May	100	387,800	115,600	30
Total	734	3,119,800	568,700	18% av.

Table 2: RAF night fighters, January–May 1941

Month	Sorties		Detections		Combats		Claims*		Total
	Night fighters	Day fighters	AI	Visual	AI	Visual	AI	Visual	
January		402		34	9			3	3
	84		44		2				
February		421		33	9	2			4
	147		25		4			2	
March		735		34	25	15			22
	270		95	20	21	10		7	
April		842		45		39	28		48.5
	342		117	10	50	5		20.5	
May		1,345		154		116	37		96
	643		204	13	74	6		59	
Totals:	1,486	3,745	485	343	151	219	82	91.5	173.5

It should be noted that some of the claims which resulted from 'visual' contact were made by AI-equipped fighters.

**Table 3: Index of Ministry of Supply output of war-stores, August 1940–May 1941
(Based on an average of four months September–December 1939 = 100)**

August	245
September	217
October	245
November	242
December	239
January	244
February	266
March	303
April	284
May	319

Table 4: Arrivals of shipping in 'foreign trade' at UK ports, 1940–41 (net tonnage)

Period	West coast ports	East and south coast ports	Total
1st Qtr 1940	2,407,000	2,655,000	5,062,000
2nd Qtr 1940	2,873,000	2,525,000	5,398,000
3rd Qtr 1940	2,614,000	869,000	3,483,000
4th Qtr 1940	2,206,000	598,000	2,804,000
1st Qtr 1941	1,799,000	727,000	2,526,000
2nd Qtr 1941	1,860,000	741,000	2,601,000
3rd Qtr 1941	2,031,000	742,000	2,773,000
4th Qtr 1941	2,080,000	677,000	2,757,000

St Dunstan in the East, City of London. The church, destroyed in the Blitz, was never rebuilt and a garden was laid out around the ruins instead. Today, it remains the most beautiful reminder of the Blitz of 1940–41. (Andrea Pucci, Getty)

BIBLIOGRAPHY AND FURTHER READING

Behrens, C.B.A., *Merchant Shipping and the Demands of War*, London, HMSO, 1955
Central Statistical Office, *Statistical Digest of the War*, London, HMSO, 1951
Churchill, Winston S., *Their Finest Hour*, London, Cassell, 1949
Collier, Basil, *The Defence of the United Kingdom*, London, HMSO, 1962
Douglas of Kirtleside, 1st Baron, *Despatch*, London, London Gazette, 1948
Goss, Chris, *The Luftwaffe's Blitz*, Manchester, Crécy, 2010. One of few books to give 'the other side' of the Blitz story.
Hooton, E.R., *Eagle in Flames: The Fall of the Luftwaffe*, London, Cassell, 1997
Jones, R.V., *Most Secret War*, London, Hamish Hamilton, 1978
Murray, Williamson, *Luftwaffe: Strategy for Defeat*, Royston, Eagle Editions, 2001
O'Brien, T.H., *Civil Defence*, London, HMSO, 1955
Overy, Richard, *The Bombing War*, London, Penguin, 2013. Professor Overy's book devotes two chapters to the Blitz.
Pile, Sir Frederick, *Despatch*, London, London Gazette, 1947
Postan, M.M., *British War Production*, London, HMSO, 1952
Price, Alfred, *Instruments of Darkness* (Revised Edition), Barnsley, Frontline, 2017. Together with R.V. Jones's *Most Secret War*, Price's book is one of the best overviews of the electronic war waged during the Blitz campaign.
Ramsey, Winston G., ed., *The Blitz Then and Now, Volume 2*, London, Battle of Britain Prints, 1988. A day-by-day account of the main Blitz period, in the 'Then and Now' style favoured by *After the Battle*.
Ray, John, *The Night Blitz*, Castle Books, London, 2004. An overview of the campaign.
Todman, Daniel, *Britain's War: Into Battle, 1937–1941*, London, Penguin, 2016
Trevor-Roper, Hugh, ed., *Hitler's War Directives 1939–1945*, London, Sidgwick & Jackson, 1964
Various, *Germany and the Second World War, Volume II: Germany's Initial Conquests in Europe*, OUP, Oxford, 2015
Various, *RAF Historical Society Journals*
White, Ian, *The History of Air Intercept Radar and the British Nightfighter 1935–1959*, Barnsley, Pen & Sword, 2007. A comprehensive history of its subject.

Air Historical Branch histories
The Air Defence of Great Britain, Vol III, Night Air Defence, June 1940–December 1941
Armament Vol II Guns, Gunsights, Turrets, Ammunition and Pyrotechnics Decoy and Deception
Signals, Vol VII, Radio Counter-Measures, 1950

USAF historical studies
Deichmann, General der Flieger Paul, *The System of Target Selection Applied by the German Air Force in World War II*
Nielsen, Generalleutnant Andreas L., *The Collection and Evaluation of Intelligence for the German Air Force High Command*

Royal Air Force Air Historical Branch (translations of German documents)
AHB Translation VII-21: Führer Directives concerning Operation *Seelöwe*
AHB Translation VII-26: Studies by the German AHB on the Campaign Against the UK
AHB Translation VII-30: Proposal for the Conduct of Air Warfare Against Britain
AHB Translation VII-39: Battle of Britain Directives by Reichsmarschall Hermann Göring
AHB Translation VII-107: Luftwaffe Strengths
AHB Translation VII-121: The Battle of Britain by Adolf Galland

The National Archives
AIR 27, Squadron Operations Record Books
AIR 50, Combat Reports
CAB 66, Cabinet Résumés, 1940–41
CAB 67/9/44, Memorandum on Air Raids on London, September–November 1940
HO 203, Home Security Reports

Websites
United States Holocaust Memorial Museum

INDEX